GLOBETROTTER™

Travel Guide

THE AZORES

TERRY MARSH

NEW
HOLLAND

NEW
HOLLAND

★★★ Highly recommended
★★ Recommended
★ See if you can

First edition published in 2009
by New Holland Publishers (UK) Ltd
London • Cape Town • Sydney • Auckland
10 9 8 7 6 5 4 3 2 1
website: www.newhollandpublishers.com

Garfield House, 86 Edgware Road
London W2 2EA, United Kingdom

80 McKenzie Street
Cape Town 8001, South Africa

Unit 1, 66 Gibbes Street, Chatswood
NSW 2067, Australia

218 Lake Road, Northcote,
Auckland, New Zealand

Distributed in the USA by
The Globe Pequot Press
Connecticut

Keep us Current
Information in travel guides is apt to change, which is
why we regularly update our guides. We'd be grateful
to receive feedback if you've noted something we
should include in our updates. If you have new information, please share it with us by writing
to the Publishing Manager, Globetrotter, at the office
nearest to you (addresses on this page). The most
significant contribution to each new edition will
receive a free copy of the updated guide.

Publishing Manager: Thea Grobbelaar
DTP Cartographic Manager: Genené Hart
Editor: Carla Zietsman
Cartographer: Reneé Spocter
Design and DTP: Nicole Bannister
Consultant: William Gray
Proofreader: Thea Grobbelaar

Reproduction Resolution, Cape Town
Printed and bound by Times Offset (M) Sdn. Bhd.,
Malaysia.

This guidebook has been written by independent
authors and updaters. The information therein represents their impartial opinion, and neither they nor the
publishers accept payment in return for including in
the book or writing more favourable reviews of any
of the establishments. Whilst every effort has been
made to ensure that this guidebook is as accurate
and up to date as possible, please be aware that the
facts quoted are subject to change, particularly the
price of food, transport and accommodation. The
Publisher accepts no responsibility or liability for any
loss, injury or inconvenience incurred by readers or
travellers using this guide.

Acknowlegdements:
Travel writers spend much time working in isolation,
but the completion of a book of this size depends on
the help of others. In particular, the willing assistance
of the following must be acknowledged:
Jorge Alves, Assistant Director, Holiday Inn, Ponta
Delgada, São Miguel, who rendered invaluable assistance and carried out much updating research into the
economics, population and politics of the islands…
…and the English-speaking taxi drivers without whom
so much would have been missed, and from whom so
much was learned (see page 126 for a list).
Finally, my thanks and my love go to my wife,
Vivienne, for looking after our dog (Teal), and for
repainting the kitchen, re-tiling the kitchen floor, and
re-roofing and creosoting the garden shed in my
absence…and for simply being one of the nicest
people anyone could ever wish to meet.

Photographic credits:
Imagebroker/Photo Access: cover;
Jonarnoldimages.com: page 108; **Terry Marsh:** title page,
pages 4, 7, 9, 11, 16, 20, 21, 26, 30, 31, 33, 35, 36, 38,
40, 41, 44, 46, 47, 49–52, 57, 59–61, 65, 68, 71–73, 75,
76, 78, 81, 82, 84, 85, 88, 92, 94–96, 98, 101,
104–106, 110, 113, 114, 116, 119, 120; **Doug
Perrine/naturepl.com/Photo Access:** page 12; **Pictures
Colour Library:** pages 19, 22, 25, 54, 103.

Cover: *Pico Island and Volcano viewed from Faial.*
Title Page: *Praça Gonçalo Velho Cabral and town
gates, Ponta Delgada.*

CONTENTS

FAROL DA PONTA DA BARCA

1
Introducing the Azores

Nine islands, nine passions, nine ways of life – the Azores are nine unique worlds, one breathtaking location.

Adrift in mid-Atlantic somewhere between Europe and America, the Azores are a seemingly distant land, off the beaten track. Yet those who visit will discover that this is a place where elemental nature plays a major role, where the scenery and the vastness of the ocean induce silent awe, and the flora and fauna are both exquisite and beguiling. And, should more ingredients be needed, the warmth of the people and the gentleness of the climate cultivate a longing to return from the moment of arrival.

On the jetty of the old pier in Santa Cruz das Flores a young boy is fishing with a bamboo pole and twine. The water is so clear he can see the fish he wants. He places the bait carefully in front of it. The fish bites, and is promptly hoicked onto land. Lunch. Simple. And yet, in its innocence, it is so characteristic of the way of life in the Azores. There is a relationship with nature that cannot be ignored, something that is part of everyday life.

These charismatic, fabled islands are a land of romance, of pirates and privateers, of novels, even television soaps, a sentimentalist's paradise that is hard to resist. Yet few people can say with conviction exactly where the Azores are to be found.

The richness of the islands' volcanic soil produces wines and liqueurs that grace tables across Europe; the lush vegetation embraces blue and green lagoons and

TOP ATTRACTIONS

*** The entire island of **Flores**.
*** **Whale** and **dolphin watching**.
*** The **Capelinhos volcano**, **Faial:** moving and memorable.
*** **Sete Cidades**, **São Miguel:** lake-filled volcanic crater.
*** **Furnas, São Miguel:** eat sweet corn cooked in boiling volcanic water, and a stew-like lunch baked in earth pits.
** **Furna do Enxofre, Graciosa:** huge sulphur cavern.
** **Angra do Heroísmo, Terceira:** World Heritage Site.
** The *fajãs* of **São Jorge:** remarkable isolated villages.

Opposite: *The Ponta da Barca lighthouse on Graciosa is a prominent landmark.*

Population: 243,018 (2006)
São Miguel: 132,671
Terceira: 55,697
Faial: 15,426
Pico: 14,806
São Jorge: 9504
Santa Maria: 5549
Graciosa: 4838
Flores: 4059
Corvo: 468
Area: 2355km^2 (909 sq miles)
São Miguel: 759km^2
  (293 sq miles)
Pico: 446km^2 (172 sq miles)
Terceira: 382km^2 (147 sq miles)
São Jorge: 246km^2 (95 sq miles)
Faial: 173km^2 (67 sq miles)
Flores: 143km^2 (55 sq miles)
Santa Maria: 97km^2
  (37 sq miles)
Graciosa: 62km^2 (24 sq miles)
Corvo: 17km^2 (6.5 sq miles)
Unemployment: The level of
unemployment varies from
island to island, but overall is
less than 4%; wage levels,
however, are low, and the
national (Portuguese) minimum
wage is € 403 per month, but
in the Azores is € 423.15
(5% more) (2007).
Religion: The majority religion
is Roman Catholic, with a
number of minor religions,
especially on the smaller
islands.
Currency: Euro (€).
Temperature: The average
temperatures range between
13°C (55°F) in winter and
24°C (75°F) in summer.

warm wispy waterfalls that are so easy on the eye you can feel your body relax in an instant; the unfathomable sea yields both gastronomic riches and nature's wonders, not least the breathtaking sight of sperm and pilot whales and skittish dolphins. Not surprisingly, once you get to know the place, you find yourself inclining to those who take the view that the Azores are the tip of the fabled, long-lost Atlantis; there is something otherworldly about the Azores. Whatever the truth, an aura of mystery hangs over this verdant string of islands – dramatic mountains and fecund valleys lush with exotic plants, dormant volcanoes, emerald green fields and meadows bounded by hydrangea and bamboo, and nine magnificent coastlines punctuated by attractive villages and towns of some antiquity.

That the Azores arose from the fiery depths of the Atlantic is not in doubt; the islands' volcanic origins are everywhere to be seen. Of Pico, for example, it was said: 'The intervention of Man did not affect the natural landscape "because from the stone, upon the same stone, a different arrangement of the stone occurred. Stone it was and stone it remained".' Elsewhere, as on São Miguel, muddy cauldrons, geysers and hot rocks are the tell-tale hallmark of a volcanic undercurrent that (hopefully) is now at rest. On Faial the most recent volcanic upheaval has left handiwork all too readily seen; in fact, Faial grew larger as a result.

As far flung from parental Portugal as can be, it is perhaps ironic that the highest mountain in all Portugal is Pico, here among the Azores; this shapely volcanic cone rises 2351m (7713ft) above sea level on the island that bears its name. That's political geography for you; the westernmost point of Portugal is here, too, on the florid island of Flores (well, to be precise, a small rock just off the coast, the Ilhéu de Monchique). But this pub quiz trivia pales against the colours and sounds of an island nation that is as distinctive and charismatic as any in Europe.

Left: *Layers of time: a vulcanologist's dream – superb deposits of multi-hued volcanic strata on the northwest coast of Graciosa.*

THE LAND

The origin of the name Azores is derived from the archaic Portuguese word *azures*, the plural of the word 'blue'. Some accounts suggest that the islands were named after the goshawk, an agile bird of prey (*açor* in Portuguese). But since the goshawk never existed in the Azores, historians now take the view that this is an unlikely explanation. As a group, the island people are fiercely independent and unique with parochial sentiments, loyalties and traditions. But they are also one, the Açores.

The nine major Azorean islands and the eight small Formigas are spread over some 600km (375 miles) of an ocean that is between 1000m and 3000m (3281ft and 9843ft) deep, and roughly 1500km (940 miles) from Lisbon. The islands of the Azores run along a northwest–southeast axis between latitudes 36–39°N and longitudes 25–31°W. The nine islands fall into three distinct groups: the **eastern islands** of São Miguel and Santa Maria; the **central islands** comprising Terceira, Graciosa, São Jorge, Pico and Faial; and the **western islands** of Flores and Corvo forming the western edge of Portugal.

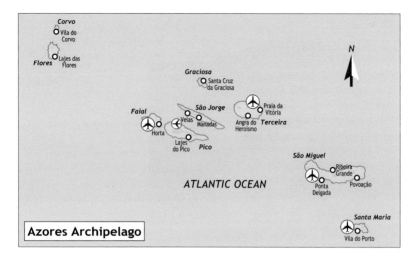

Azores Archipelago

Part of the eastern group of islands, the **Formigas** are located northeast of Santa Maria and southeast of São Miguel. *Formigas* is Portuguese for 'ants', because the islets are many and small, some being little more than rocks in the ocean. Nevertheless, the islets are useful for navigation, visible up to 19km (12 miles) away on a clear day. There are no animals or plants on the Formigas, but they have special biological interest and are a nature reserve.

All the islands of the Azores are volcanic in origin, and are essentially the tips of volcanoes, some of the tallest mountains on the planet, as measured from their base at the bottom of the ocean, although remarkably little is known about their geological origins. Deep down on the ocean bed three tectonic plates meet, somewhere between Faial and Flores: the islands of Flores and Corvo actually lie on a different plate, the North American, from the rest of the islands. No-one knows whether the central and eastern islands lie on the Eurasian or African plates, or, indeed, whether they sit on a mini-plate of their own. It all makes for exciting geology characterized by occasional seismic tremors, which, scientists confirm, occur almost daily, but at a level too insubstantial to be noticed out on the streets.

Volcanic eruptions have occurred within recent historical times, but the volcanoes on the islands of Corvo, Flores and Santa Maria are now thought to be dormant. The last volcano to erupt was the **Capelinhos Volcano** (*Vulcão dos Capelinhos*) in 1957, in the western part of Faial, increasing the size of that island. In the past, eruptions occurred on Pico (1562–64, 1718 and 1720); São Miguel (Lagoa do Fogo: 1563–64); Faial (1672–73), and São Jorge (1808).

As for earthquakes, the most devastating happened centuries apart: in 1522 an earthquake destroyed Vila Franca do Campo, until then the capital of São Miguel. Another quake shattered the city of Angra do Heroísmo on Terceira as recently as 1980, and yet one more had serious consequences for the island of Faial in 1998.

The Climate

Surrounded by a huge expanse of ocean warmed by the Gulf Stream, the Azores enjoy a mild and equable climate, and are a pleasure to visit throughout the year. The **temperature in winter** almost never reaches freezing at coast level, and only produces a frost above 1000m (3280ft). In **summer**, the temperature can rise to 27°C (81°F), but seldom any higher.

There is **rainfall** in every month, but it is rarely a driving, penetrating rain; for the most part it is not long lasting (but occasionally is), and you can frequently drive through rain showers into brilliant sunshine. There is a local saying that

---

SATA — THE WINGS OF A DREAM

The airline SATA Internacional is the realization of a dream to link the islands of the Azores, bringing them closer to each other and linking them with the outside world. The company began in 1947, and in that same year acquired its first aircraft, a Beechcraft called *Açor*, and on 15 June 1947 made its maiden flight between São Miguel and Santa Maria, transporting seven passengers and two crew members.

Left: *The radiance of an early morning rainbow, Santa Cruz, Flores.*

you can see all four seasons in one day, and the weather is so changeable that a morning of rain can clear the air for an afternoon of sunshine. **Humidity** is usually within a narrow range, 80–85%, but can increase to 100%, which explains the island's lush vegetation.

Sea temperatures are ideal for swimming throughout the year, and vary from around 15°C (59°F) in February to a high of 24°C (75°F) in August and September. As with many parts of the world, weather patterns are becoming less predictable. June and July, however, are still the warmest months; April and September the least stable. But the Azores, as regards climate, remain a place you can visit at any time of the year.

Natura 2000: Protecting the Azores Environment

Natura 2000 is an ecological network operating in the European Union. In May 1992, the governments of the EU adopted legislation designed to protect the most seriously threatened habitats and species across Europe. This legislation is called the **Habitats Directive** and complements the **Birds Directive** adopted in 1979. These two Directives are the basis of the creation of the Natura 2000 network, and there are many sites across the Azores which fall within the ambit of Natura 2000.

The Birds Directive requires the establishment of Special Protection Areas (SPAs) for birds. The Habitats Directive similarly requires Special Areas of Conservation (SACs) to be designated for other species and for habitats. Together, SPAs and SACs make up the Natura 2000 sites.

The Natura 2000 network contributes to the 'Emerald network' of Areas of Special Conservation Interest (ASCIs) set up under the Bern Convention on the conservation of European wildlife and natural habitats.

Each EU Member State must compile a list of the best wildlife areas containing the habitats and species listed in the Habitats Directive and the Birds Directive. This list must then be submitted to the European Commission, after which an evaluation and selection process on a European level will take place in order to become a Natura 2000 site. Pico da Vara on São Miguel is one such site.

Flora and Fauna

The Azores is a true paradise for nature lovers, offering dramatic landscapes and lush and colourful vegetation that benefits from the rainfall, humidity, as well as the position of the islands and their volcanic soil. On all nine islands there are dozens of natural reserves, protected landscape areas, parks and forests. Many tropical species thrive here alongside European plants with the result that there is a hotchpotch of colour and vibrancy, and a bizarre but agreeable mix of beech, pine, cedar, juniper, tropical ferns and palms along with sequoia, dragon tree, jacaranda and the **Japanese cryptomeria** (cedar), which lines lava gullies and is grown commercially on some islands. The hydrangea is the most emblematic flower, growing here in abundance and used to demarcate field boundaries, but there is also a colourful spread of azalea, hibiscus, belladonna lily, and African lily, more extensively flourishing on Madeira.

Once a dense evergreen forest covered the islands, but this has long been cleared for farming and settlement. There is still some native vegetation, in isolated areas, and a few remnant patches of the original forest. The largest

Below: *The beautiful belladonna lily grows in profusion on most islands, but is especially abundant on Flores, where it is often used as a dinner table decoration.*

area is on Terceira, on the **Caldeira de Santa Bárbara**. The only remaining **natural forest** on São Miguel is at the eastern end of the island on Pico da Vara. Although most of the plant species have been introduced, the islands remain a place of endless fascination to plant lovers. Of almost 1000 species, only around 300 are regarded as native, of which as few as 60 or so are classed as endemic, found only in the Azores.

The nearest thing to anything that is going to do you harm are rats, ferrets, rabbits and hedgehogs; the Azores harbour nothing more lethal, as animals go.

Although some 150 species of **bird** have been recorded on the islands, most are species found in mainland Europe (although there is always the possibility of an exotic migrant being blown off-course), and there are a number of subspecies peculiar to the Azores. Out at sea the bird to watch out for is **Cory's shearwater**, skimming low over the waves. **Common tern** and **roseate tern** also put in a regular appearance; inland you can expect to find common buzzard, goldcrest (of which there are three distinct subspecies on the islands), collared dove, rock pigeon, grey wagtail (slightly different from its mainland European or Madeiran counterpart), and canary. The real

Right: *Bottlenose dolphin are common around the Azores.*

treat, and hard to find, is the grey **Azorean bullfinch** (*Pyrrhula murina*), once common on the islands, but shot almost to extinction, mainly by fruit farmers who also regarded blackbird, canary and blackcap as pests. Anyone looking for the bullfinch should head for the Nature Reserve on Pico da Vara on São Miguel.

Offshore the probability of encountering **whales** or **dolphins** is so good that the local companies that run boat trips looking for them offer a money-back guarantee if they don't find anything. Whales and dolphins are cetaceans, a word derived from the Greek for 'sea monster'. There are more than 80 species worldwide, 25 of which have been sighted off the Azores.

Commercial **whaling** was an important part of the islands' economy for many years, but all that has now ended. The location of the Azores, in the mid-Atlantic, and with steep-sided islands that create upwellings of cold water from the depths to the surface where they meet the warm waters of the Gulf Stream to create a nutrient-rich feeding ground for whales, is perfect. The most common species found around the islands is the **sperm whale**, which is easily identifiable from a distance as its blow-hole is to one side of its head, sending spray into the air at an angle, compared with all other whales that have blow-holes centrally placed on top of their heads. **Pilot whales**, **beaked** and **bottlenose whales** turn up from time to time, as do **killer whales** on passage. Happily, some of the great whales are returning to Azorean waters, including the **humpback** and **blue whale**. The most common **dolphins** are the bottlenose, common, Risso's, striped and Atlantic spotted.

HISTORY IN BRIEF

The islands were known in the 14th century when they appeared, incompletely, on the **Atlas Catalan** published in 1375, and were mentioned in several accounts of voyages, and it appears that the Azores were discovered between 1317 and 1339 by Portuguese and Genoese sailors. But, echoing the same spin-doctoring that applied to Madeira's Islands, they were only 'officially' discovered many years later, in 1427, when **Santa Maria** is said to have been the

SCRIMSHAW

Scrimshaw is the name given to handiwork created by whalers most commonly using the bones and teeth of sperm whales and the baleen of other whales. It takes the form of elaborate carvings of pictures and lettering on the surface of the bone or tooth, with the engravings highlighted using a pigment. The making of scrimshaw began on whaling ships between 1817 and 1824, and survived until the ban on commercial whaling. The practice survives as a hobby and as a trade for commercial artisans. A maker of scrimshaw is known as a *scrimshander*. Scrimshaw is derived from the shipboard practice of sailors using simple tools and materials to hand, and on whaling ships the by-products of whales were readily available. Whale bone is ideally suited for the task, as it is easy to work and was very plentiful. Scrimshaw essentially was a leisure activity for whalers. Because whalers were unable to work at night, they had more free time than other sailors. A lot of scrimshaw was never signed and a great many of the pieces are anonymous. Early scrimshaw was done with crude sailing needles, and candle black, soot or tobacco juice would have been used to bring the etched design into view. **Warning**: It is not illegal to make or sell scrimshaw – indeed many shops make a trade in selling scrimshaw artefacts and jewellery – but it is illegal to transport it from the Azores. If found at Customs on your return, scrimshaw will be confiscated.

first to be found, by one of the captains sailing for Henry the Navigator, possibly Gonçalo Velho, but this is not certain. The uncertainty arises because Captain Gonçalo Velho is also credited with landing, 12 years later, on São Miguel, on the sands of Povoação, and at this period reliable historians were thin on the ground.

King Alfonso V ordered the colonization of the then unoccupied islands, starting in 1439, with people mainly from the continental provinces of Estremadura, the Algarve and Alentejo, and later on from Madeira and Morocco. At this time, the capital of the islands was at **Vila Franca do Campo**, an area then as now surrounded by fertile land, and with a decent harbour. Ponta Delgada and Ribeira Grande were also founded as a consequence of settlement expanding along the coast in search of suitable land. By 1452 all the islands had been 'discovered', but not all were settled immediately: **Terceira** in 1450, **Pico** and **Faial** 16 years later, **Graciosa** and **São Jorge** in 1480, but another century was to elapse before the most remote of the islands, **Flores** and **Corvo**, were settled. As in Madeira, each of the islands was subject to the command of a donee-captain, who had responsibility for settling the islands and for their development.

The Azores played an important part in the history of Portugal, particularly in the conquest and defence of Portuguese strongholds in North Africa. They were also a convenient stop-over for shipping from India, and supported the expeditions heading off to explore the Americas.

The virtual destruction of Vila Franca do Campo by an earthquake in 1522 foreshadowed difficulties for São Miguel. In 1563, another eruption had disastrous consequences for the area around Ribeira Grande.

In 1583, **Philip II of Spain** as king of Portugal sent his combined Iberian fleet to clear the French traders from the Azores, decisively hanging his prisoners of war from the yardarms and fuelling the so-called 'Black Legend', a term coined by Julián Juderías in his 1914 book *La leyenda negra y la verdad histórica* (*The Black Legend and Historical Truth*) to describe the unfair and biased depiction of Spain and Spaniards as cruel, intolerant and

NATURE THROUGH

Life in the Azores is relaxed and taken at an easy pace; impatience will get you nowhere. Just go with the flow, travel slowly, and enjoy the calmness of life. The easiest way to travel between the islands is by air, but they are also linked by ferry from May to October, while the islands of Faial, Pico and São Jorge have a year-round ferry. Arriving by ferry makes a more leisurely approach, accompanied by the chance of spotting dolphin or even whale...or maybe just feeling the sea breeze in your hair.

5,000,000BP Santa Maria appears, and disappears.
1,000,000BP Santa Maria reappears along with eastern part of São Miguel.
300,000BP Western São Miguel (Sete Cidades) appears, along with Pico. The remaining islands appear between 1,000,000 and 300,000 years BP. The islands remained pristine until the 15th century; no-one had ever settled here.
c1427 The first recorded landfalls in the Azores, on Santa Maria.
c1439 São Miguel settled, and the remaining islands progressively 'discovered' and settled; Corvo was the last to be populated.
1440–1957 Years dominated by volcanic eruptions – São Miguel (1440, 1563); Pico (1562, 1718, 1720); Faial (1672, 1957), São Jorge (1808) – but also by much building, especially in the 16th and 17th centuries.

1522 The virtual destruction of Vila Franca do Campo by earthquake foreshadowed difficulties for São Miguel.
1563 Volcanic eruption with disastrous consequences around Ribeira Grande.
1580 Portugal is annexed to Spain.
1583 Philip II of Spain, as king of Portugal, sends his Iberian fleet to clear the French traders from the Azores.
1640 Portugal regains independence from Spain.
1751 First recorded export of oranges.
1811 A new island appears off the coast of São Miguel, but soon afterwards, having been 'claimed' for the British, sinks beneath the sea.
1820 Civil war in Portugal.
1820 Cultivation of tea first introduced by Jacinto Leite.
1870 Whale hunting begins in the Azores.
1893 Telegraphic cable laid between Faial and Lisbon.

1943 Portuguese dictator António de Oliveira Salazar leases bases in the Azores to the British.
1944 American forces constructs a small and short-lived air base on the island of Santa Maria.
1945 A new base founded on the island of Terceira, known as Lajes Field.
1957 Major volcanic activity at Capelinhos on Faial, resulting in loss of life, destruction of property and the growth in size of the island.
1976 The Azores declared an Autonomous Region with an Assembly and a Regional Government.
1980 Earthquake hits Terceira, and also affects São Jorge and Graciosa.
1981 Whale hunting ceases; many islanders leave for North America following the 1980 earthquake.
1998 Earthquake damages a large part of Faial.

fanatical throughout history. The second-to-last part of the Portuguese empire to resist Philip's reign over Portugal, the Azores were returned to Portuguese control, not by military force, but by the people attacking a well-fortified Castilian garrison.

With the recovery of Portugal's independence in 1640, new horizons opened up for **São Miguel**. But this coincided with a time when the techniques of dyeing with woad (grown on São Miguel and elsewhere among the islands) were being substituted by the use of indigo from the Americas, and this eventually led to the cultivation of woad being abandoned. Unfortunately, the growing of substitute crops, mainly wheat and flax, did not compensate for the loss of income from woad, and the economic life of São Miguel became increasingly difficult.

São Miguel only recovered its economic position by producing and exporting **oranges**. No-one is certain when oranges were first introduced into the Azores, but it is thought to have been around the mid-16th century. The first recorded export of oranges is dated 1751, and comprised just three crates, sent to Britain. But by 20 years later, exports were a regular feature, expanding considerably to reach a peak of 17,400 crates between 1790 and the end of the century. The importance of the orange, however, was brought to an end when the orange trees were wiped out by disease.

The 1820 civil war in Portugal had strong repercussions in the Azores. In 1829, in Vila da Praia, the Liberals won over the Absolutists, making Terceira the main headquarters of the new Portuguese regime and establishing there the Council of Regency of Mary II of Portugal.

Beginning in 1868, Portugal issued its stamps overprinted with 'AÇORES' for use in the islands. Between 1892 and 1906, it also issued separate stamps for the three administrative districts of the time.

From 1836 to 1976, the archipelago was divided into

Right: *Street sign, Ponta Delgada, commemorating the first President of the Azores Autonomous Region.*

Left: *The Azores flag.*

three **districts**, equivalent to those in the Portuguese mainland. The division was arbitrary, and did not follow natural island groups, but reflected the location of each district capital on the three main cities:

Angra consisted of Terceira, São Jorge, and Graciosa, with the capital at Angra do Heroísmo on Terceira.

Horta consisted of Pico, Faial, Flores, and Corvo, with the capital at Horta on Faial.

Ponta Delgada consisted of São Miguel and Santa Maria, with the capital at Ponta Delgada on São Miguel.

Towards the end of the 19th century, several scientists, including Prince Albert I of Monaco, deduced that the Azores anticyclone had a major influence on the weather in western Europe, concluding that if information on the anticyclone could be transmitted rapidly to the mainland, the weather could be forecast days ahead of time. As a result, in 1893, a telegraphic cable was laid between Faial and Lisbon, so bringing the **weather forecast** into being.

Between 1900 and 1928, Horta on Faial became an important anchoring point for **underwater transatlantic** cables, with the result that American, English, French, German and Italian companies all employed staff to work on Faial. The present-day Faial Hotel is actually housed in the Western Union building from this era. By 1960, with improvements in radio telephone communications, the use of the cable had ceased.

TOPLESS SUNBATHING

Topless sunbathing by women is not something seen in the Azores. It is not prohibited, but is simply not part of the culture. However, casual observation around the islands suggests that there is only a matter of millimetres between observing the culture and actually being topless.

While São Miguel is clearly the principal destination, Terceira likes to muscle in on the act on the strength of the fact that it serves as a hub for inter-island flights, as well as some international flights. The pity is that not all the islands get a fair crack of the tourism whip. In this regard Flores and Corvo lose out most because of suggestions that they are inaccessible; remote; that if you get there the weather may prevent you from returning; that there are no adequate facilities, and so on. The reality is that bad weather can prevent you from getting to any of the islands, but it is rare that flights have to be cancelled on that account. Facilities do exist on Flores and Corvo, and, not to put too fine a point on it, Flores is quite simply the most scenically beautiful of all the islands. No trip to the Azores would be complete without a visit to Flores. The trouble is: visit Flores and you may never want to leave.

Altogether, the Azores are a beautiful and endearing place of culture, charm and cuisine, and, for the time being, largely unknown and pristine. Tourism management policies will ensure that it remains pristine; tourists who enjoy natural beauty and nature in the raw will do the rest, and, if you are reading this book, then you, hopefully, are about to become one of the elite who know what a wonderful destination these islands are.

During World War II, in 1943, Portuguese dictator António de Oliveira Salazar leased bases in the Azores to the British. This represented a change in policy: previously the Portuguese government allowed only German U-boats and navy ships to refuel there. This was a key turning point in the Battle of the Atlantic, allowing the Allies to provide aerial coverage in the middle of the Atlantic. This helped them to hunt U-boats and protect convoys.

In 1944, **American forces** constructed a small and short-lived air base on the island of Santa Maria. In 1945, a new base was founded on the island of Terceira and is currently known as **Lajes Field**, built on a broad, flat sea terrace that had been a farm, a plateau rising out of the sea on the northeast corner of the island.

During the Cold War, the US Navy anti-submarine squadrons patrolled the North Atlantic for Soviet submarines and surface spy vessels. Since its inception, Lajes Field has been used for refuelling aircraft bound for Europe and, more recently, the Middle East. The US Army operates a small fleet of military ships in the harbour of Praia da Vitória, 3km (2 miles) southeast of Lajes Field.

GOVERNMENT AND ECONOMY

In 1976, the Azores became the **Autonomous Region of the Azores** (*Região Autónoma dos Açores*), one of the autonomous regions of Portugal, and the Azorean districts were suppressed. Since becoming a Portuguese Autonomous Region, the executive section of the local authority has been located in Ponta Delgada, the legislative in Horta and the judicial in Angra do Heroísmo, although each island has its own judicial system.

Azorean politics are dominated by the two largest Portuguese political parties – **PSD** (*Partido Social Democrata*) and **PS** (*Partido Socialista*), the latter holding a majority in the Regional Legislative Assembly. The **PP** (*Partido Popular*) is also represented in the local parliament, in coalition with the PSD. Even though the PS dominates the administrative scene, the PSD is usually more popular in city and town council elections.

The Economy

Tourism, fishing and agriculture (beef and dairy products) are the mainstay of the global island economy, with island variations. Dairy cattle abound; in fact, on São Miguel it is said that cattle outnumber people almost three to one. There was a time when oranges were the principal product from the islands, but now it is **pineapples**, which are grown organically in large greenhouses. São Miguel also produces **tea** and **tobacco** for cigarettes and cigars. **Wine**, too, has its place, and vineyards dot the islands, notably Pico. Fishing is also important, and large quantities of Portuguese tuna are fished in Azorean waters.

Today, tourism is the major growth area, and high quality, luxury hotels are appearing around the main centres on São Miguel and Terceira, and on some of the more remote islands. Tour operators are increasingly interested in the Azores as a destination, and, since flights to all the islands have become possible, it makes the whole archipelago a viable holiday destination. Even so, there is no question that for the foreseeable future the Azores need the income from tourism, and not only in the peak months of July and August (even then most hotels have more than 90% occupancy only in August); visitors out of the main season can do much to help those who genuinely want to promote the islands as a tourist destination, many of whom have to earn enough in two months to last for 12.

Ironically, interest from Portugal, the most obvious contender for holidays in the Azores, was aroused only after a popular television soap programme began filming on the island (*see* panel, page 21). More needs to be done to bring tourists to this remarkably equable climate at other times of the year, when

The cultivation of tea was first introduced in the Azores by Jacinto Leite around 1820. Jacinto began the first plantation in São Miguel using seeds brought from Brazil where he was stationed as Commander of the Royal Guards. During the 19th century, the decline of the orange trade allowed space for the production of tea, which reached its peak in the 1850s, producing 250 tons per 300ha. But World War I and protectionist policies that favoured the tea producers of Mozambique led to a decline in the tea industry of the Azores, and now only two manufacturers survive. The Azores are the only tea-producing area in Europe.

Below: *Much of the tea in Europe's only tea-producing country comes from the Gorreana tea factory on São Miguel.*

Above: *It is not unusual to find donkeys being used as a form of transport.*

prices are lower. The cost of living is already significantly less than in mainland Europe, and certainly much less so than in the UK; car fuel, for example, is half the cost it is in the UK, France and Germany.

But there has been considerable investment from Europe, and many of the roads are in excellent condition across all the islands, with an ongoing programme of road improvement everywhere. On each island, except Corvo, there are road transport services (albeit geared rather more to locals' needs than tourists') and taxis. You can rent cars on the eight main islands, and there are car tours of Corvo for those that need them. As well as the new hotels that are appearing, excellent restaurants serving traditional cuisine are sprouting in some of the most idyllic settings.

But there is a long way to go before the Azores become a thronged tourist destination. For the moment, this is a peaceful compendium of individually unique yet unified holiday resorts, expanding slowly but positively. In essence, however, the Azores are largely underdeveloped in that particular market, and it is hoped they will never succumb to the level of tourist invasion that bedevils some of the Mediterranean islands, or even further south in the Canary Islands. This is a wonderful, relaxing place.

THE PEOPLE

The **population** of the islands has remained fairly static, at a little over 240,000 for some years, although the latest figures suggest a slight rise. Most live in such towns and cities as there are, with the rest pursuing an agrarian lifestyle across the islands. In the past, large numbers of Azorean people emigrated, mainly to Canada, the USA and Brazil, but are returning in their retirement years, and there is some evidence that parents are returning, too, with their young children in the belief – not altogether unfounded – that the islands offer a safer way of life and a better quality of existence. There is an incidence of minor crime among the islands, but, as with most island populations, it is localized and petty.

The Language

Portuguese is the language of the Azores, although there are numerous variations in dialect, vocabulary, accent and expression as you move from island to island. It is these localized variations that make learning Portuguese fraught with difficulty, and even the people themselves acknowledge that it is a difficult language to master – anyone wanting a jeweller, for example, will have to get their tongue around *ourivesaria* (oo-reeves-a-ree-ah). In the main towns, you will find that English is spoken widely, and this is certainly the case in information centres, hotels and restaurants. Many taxi drivers speak good English; many more speak enough to get by, but some speak only Portuguese. So, it is always a good idea to have an itinerary typed out so that you can face the worst-case scenario of pointing at a list. It has to be said that even those who don't speak English are genuinely affable and keen to help.

In rural areas among the islands English is not so readily used, although you are always likely to find someone to help. Wherever there are information panels at an attraction, they are invariably in Portuguese and English, and tour guides and brochures are available in multiple languages. English is taught as a standard subject in schools, and there are a number of television channels in English.

Below: *Postboxes, São Miguel.*

Of course, it does no harm, and often a lot of good, to have just a few basic words to hand, even if it's only 'please' (*por favor*) or 'thank you' (*obrigado* for men, and *obrigada* for women); 'yes' (*sim*) or 'no' (*não*). The main thing, as with any foreign language, is not to use words you would not use in your daily life; keep it as simple as possible. The 'Travel Tips' section (*see* page 123) contains some useful words you may want to remember.

Religion

All the islands of the Azores are Catholic in their beliefs, although there are Protestant churches in Ponta Delgada, built mainly to serve the British merchants who came to the islands to manage the production of oranges.

Above: *Small chapel, Vila de Água de Pau, São Miguel.*

Traditions

The maintenance of traditions is always important, and no more so than for island communities such as the Azores. But here, as elsewhere, there is a steady erosion of cultural traditions. The traditional dress of the Azores, such as the **capote**, a cape with a large hood framed by whalebone, is now only worn during festivals, or as part of an evening's entertainment for tourists in the hotels.

The **Festivals of the Lord Christ** (*Festas do Senhor Santo Cristo*) at Ponta Delgada (São Miguel) are truly colourful and entertaining events, the St John's Festivals (*Sanjoaninas* at Angra do Heroísmo or Praia da Vitória on Terceira), with folk dancing and bullfights (*see* below), and the playing with cattle at the '*Espera do gado*', the Sea Festivals at Horta (Faial), with lively sports activities, are high points in a calendar of events that are genuinely popular and last from January to December.

Festivals, however, are a cause for celebration, and these have generally retained their importance across a global network. The people of the Azores are deeply religious and their faith is expressed through festivals, observing age-old traditions. On the fifth Sunday after Easter, Ponta Delgada celebrates **Cristo dos Milagres** which draws expat Azoreans from across the world. All the islands celebrate the **Feast of the Holy Ghost** (*Festas do Espírito Santo*) when a gift-laden emperor is elected and bright and ornate buildings – Empires of the Holy Ghost (*Império do Espírito Santo*) – found in many villages are used to house objects associated with the festival. This festival originated in the Middle Ages and is celebrated on all nine islands between May and September; it is the highlight of the social calendar for each island.

Bullfighting (*Tourada à Corda*) is not as bloody as in other parts of Europe. In the Azores, where the only blood spilt is of those who get in the way or are not nimble enough, the bull is held on a long rope by men who try to control the animal. The object is to approach the bull as closely as possible and keep away from the horns. Sometimes things get a little out of hand, but it is rare to encounter serious injury to either man or beast. Another form of bullfighting takes place on some islands, Graciosa and Terceira, for example; here the bull is stabbed in its shoulders with a blade, but is not killed.

Cultural Heritage

In a land of earthquakes, it is a wonder that any significantly old architecture survives; indeed, most of the principal buildings of antiquity date from the Baroque period, developed in the 18th century. This was a time of great wealth based on gold imported from Brazil. The few churches and buildings in which Gothic elements are present stem from the initial settlement period. With good examples of religious and civil art and architecture of the **Renaissance** and **Baroque**, the 16th and 17th centuries correspond to a golden age, a time when the Azores were a port of call for ships laden with treasures from America and the Orient.

The year-round temperate climate contributes to the islands being a perfect place for those who want to play **golf**. There are two golf courses on São Miguel and one on Terceira:
Campo de Golfe da Batalha, tel: 296 498 540, www.verdegolf.net (18 holes).
Campo de Golfe das Furnas, tel: 296 584 651, www.verdegolf.net (27 holes).
Clube de Golfe da Terceira, tel: 295 902 299, www.terceiragolf.com (18 holes).

Not surprisingly, virtually all the old buildings are fabricated from the dark volcanic rocks that were so readily available. But many of the church interiors, especially in Ponta Delgada and Angra do Heroísmo, reveal decorative splendour, with gilded altars, *azulejos*, lecterns carved from jacaranda wood and adorned with ivory.

During the 19th century, some large American dynasties that had prospered from trade or the orange plantations, built sumptuous mansions in Ponta Delgada, Furnas and Horta. Typical of this period is Thomas Hickling's palace in the centre of Ponta Delgada, now the **São Pedro Hotel**, and a style of building known disparagingly as 'Orange architecture' because it was funded by profits of orange production.

Away from the towns, the rural architecture preserves much of the islands' distinctive styles, influenced by Alentejo and the Algarve, with whitewashed houses and brightly coloured borders that frame the façades.

The abundance of churches leaves you in no doubt that this is a deeply religious nation. It has been for a long time, and no mention of Azorean architecture can be made without including ***impérios***, one of the most intriguing aspects of an age-old religion; they are simply chapels dedicated to the Holy Spirit, and are found throughout the islands, although the finest are on Terceira, where they are brightly painted and festive. The religious way of life is very important to the people of the Azores, and manifests itself in numerous processions, pilgrimages and festivals throughout the year.

Many of the islands' churches link the present with the first period of settlement, while the 16th and 17th centuries were times of intensive building programmes during which time the character of the buildings was often adapted to suit the materials to hand, as well as developing an idiosyncrasy based on the islands' remoteness from mainland Europe.

Nor has the cultural landscape been overlooked; the vineyards on the island of Pico, situated on old lava-covered fields, have been recognized by UNESCO as a World Heritage Site.

Left: *Sweet juicy pineapples for sale at Ponta Delgada Market, São Miguel.*

Food and Drink

With the Azores' nutrient-filled waters and rich fisheries, it is not surprising that fish features on every menu. There are more than 50 edible species of fish around the islands, served in almost as many different ways. Most common are grouper (*badejo*), scabbard fish (*espada*), swordfish (*espadarte*) and red mullet (*salmonete*). You can also get shellfish, clams, limpets or barnacles (*lapas*).

Cheeses from the island of São Jorge and elsewhere, sweet and juicy **pineapples** from São Miguel, small, sweet **bananas**, and the **wine** from Pico are all major items in the gastronomic menu of the Azores. Many of the other wines are imported from Portugal, notably Douro and Alentejo, which produce excellent full-bodied red wines.

The social development of São Miguel is different from the other islands, and it is bigger in area and production levels. So, three different levels of domestic cuisine evolved: the rich cuisine of the villas and big houses; the bourgeois, middle-class cuisine, and the 'poor' cuisine, characterized by the people's ingenuity in creating dishes with imagination from simple produce.

COOKING WITH
VOLCANOES

In Furnas on São Miguel, it is possible to have a local speciality, **Cozido à portuguesa**, which is actually cooked in pots buried in the hot volcanic soil for a few hours before being unearthed and rushed to the hotel restaurants for lunch. *Cozido à portuguesa* (Portuguese stew) is a rich stew made from shin of beef, pork and chicken and served with cabbage, carrots, turnips, smoked sausages and potatoes, with a number of local variations. Washed down with half a bottle of red Basafto from Pico, you have a filling and satisfying lunchtime meal.

2
São Miguel

Named the 'Green Island' (*Ilha Verde*), **São Miguel** is largely covered with fields and meadows in the lowlands, and *laurisilva* forests in the hills. Geysers and hot springs (*caldeiras*) are spread over the east of the island, which is composed of an old solid mass reaching from Povoação to Nordeste. São Miguel has a number of *caldeiras*, and three so-called stratovolcanoes – volcanoes that are characterized by a steep, cone-shaped profile and periodic eruptions: Sete Cidades, Água de Pau and Furnas. The volcanic masses are connected along a cone-like mass made up of shapely peaks. This is most evident in the area between Sete Cidades and Fogo, which geologists call a monogenetic volcanic field, here comprising no fewer than 270 volcanoes. They are primarily composed of basaltic cones formed during Strombolian and Hawaiian-style eruptions. It is the most recently active area of the island. The youngest volcanoes are relatively well dated, and it is possible to count 19 eruptions that occurred 3000 years ago.

São Miguel is said to be the location of the mythical island of Ogygia, mentioned in Homer's *Odyssey* as the home of the nymph Calypso, the daughter of the Titan, Atlas, also known as *Atlantis* in ancient Greek.

Following the initial eruption of a group of volcanoes (between 4.2 and 0.25 million years ago), another eruption occurred in the vicinity of present-day Povoação, forming the central core of the future island of São Miguel. The area formed by this upsurge was later

DON'T MISS

*** **Sete Cidades:** a vast volcanic crater filled with lakes.
*** **Furnas:** eat sweet corn cooked in boiling volcanic water, and a stew-like lunch (*cozido*) baked in earth pits.
*** **Whale watching:** do not miss a chance to go out whale and dolphin watching.
*** **Achada das Furnas:** an enchanting valley grafted into the green hills and mountains.
*** **Terra Nostra Garden:** have lunch in the restaurant and then stroll around the gardens.
** **Ponta Delgada city gates** (*Portas da Cidade*): this curious construction dates from the 18th century.

Opposite: *Chapel of Nossa Senhora da Paz.*

VITAL STATISTICS

São Miguel is the largest island in the archipelago of the Azores, and has an area of 759km² (293 sq miles) measuring approximately 81km (50 miles) long by 15.5km (9 miles) wide at the maximum points. The highest point on the island is Pico da Vara in the east at 1103m (3618ft). São Miguel has around 132,000 inhabitants (called *Micaelenses*); the largest town is Ponta Delgada, with about 30,000 inhabitants (2007).

increased by eruptions of the volcanic groups of Furnas (800,000 years ago), and Fogo (from 290,000 years ago). The emergence of the Sete Cidades massif (550,000 years ago) created another island, separated by a channel. Gradually the two islands began to join to form the present island of São Miguel 50,000 years ago.

The island draws the bulk of the tourists because of its splendid natural landscapes, attractive network of roads, many with superbly positioned **viewpoints** (*miradouro*) often complete with picnic tables and barbecues (wood supplied by the local government on a daily basis). There are no huge beaches, but those that do exist are for the most part tucked into sheltered niches among the sea cliffs. Black sand, not surprisingly, is the norm – but children seem to love it! The most popular beaches are at Pópulo and Milícias, near Ponta Delgada, where long stretches of sand are framed by lush greenery. Mosteiros has an attractive beach looking out to the small islands that bear its name – Ilhéu dos Mosteiros.

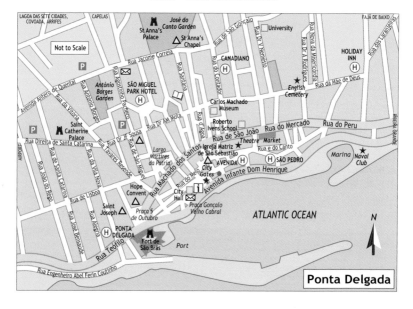

Ponta Delgada

PONTA DELGADA ★★

Formerly a simple fishing village, Ponta Delgada started to assume greater importance after the disaster at Vila Franca do Campo. This is a level, almost rectangular city about 3km (2 miles) in length, overlooking the bay, and densely populated with churches. The older part of the city is set back from the Avenida Infante Dom Henrique, a wide boulevard with traditional black-and-white pavement that parallels the harbour.

The historic centre of the city gives a keen perspective on its development, especially during the 19th century, when it attracted wealthy landowners. Many of the parks and gardens in Ponta Delgada date from this time, introduced mainly by the English.

The best way to explore Ponta Delgada is on foot, but you could also try the inexpensive tourist train, **A Lagarta**, which starts near the Fort de São Brás at the western end of the Avenida Infante Dom Henrique.

City Gates (*Portas da Cidade*) ★★

This curious construction dates from the 18th century. Composed of three tall arches, the gate is capped by a royal crown. Walk beneath the arches and you are in good company, including the Portuguese kings Don Pedro IV and Don Carlos I, as well as Prince Albert of Monaco. It is said that if you walk through the gateway just before you leave the Azores, and make a wish, either simply to return, or for something more esoteric, then your wish will be granted.

Sant'Ana Garden Park (Jácome Correia Palace) ★★

This typically 19th-century building today houses the seat of the Presidency of the Regional Government of the Azores. There are 18th- and 19th-century items of furniture and paintings, and a collection of glazed tiles. The surrounding garden is magnificent, with displays of trees, bushes, ornamental plants and a central rose garden leading up to the main doorway to the palace.

Above: *The Praça Gonçalo Velho Cabral and the nearby town gates is an agreeable and relaxing place on the edge of Ponta Delgada centre.*

City Hall ★★

A fine example of Baroque architecture, the 17th-century city hall has pyramids united in a rosary on its front. The bell tower dates from 1724, and inside is a 16th-century bell gifted by King Don João III.

Carlos Machado Museum ★

The Museu Carlos Machado was founded in 1880 and since 1930 installed in the former 16th-century Convento de Santo André. This museum is today considered one of the most notable museums of the Azores, and began with collections in natural history (particularly zoology), botany, geology and mineralogy. With sections on regional art and ethnography being added later, the importance of this museum increased considerably. When the museum was moved to the convent, the collections were further extended to include jewellery, glazed tiles, porcelain, toys, paintings, sculptures and folk art. Other artwork includes oil paintings of the Portuguese school from the 16th century, as well as the collection of contemporary art.

Fort de São Brás *

The fort was built in the 16th century, around 1552, and redeveloped in the 19th century. It is a typical Renaissance fort in spite of its later alterations, and is recognized as the most important military fort in São Miguel, being built on a promontory to defend the city against pirates and corsairs. The fortress retains the original octagonal structure, and it is today used as a base for the Portuguese navy.

Igreja Matriz de São Sebastião *

This 16th-century parish church was built on the site of a former chapel, and possesses a graceful **Manueline doorway** in white limestone brought from Portugal. Those who appreciate religious architecture will find the interior noteworthy for the chancel vaulting and the gilded Baroque statues of the Evangelists on the high altar. To the left of the chancel, the sacristy is decorated with *azulejos*, and is home to some beautifully crafted 17th-century carvings made from the wood of the jacaranda tree.

Whale Watching ***

There are numerous companies operating close by the marina in Ponta Delgada, and offering half- or full-day whale-watching tours. They are an unmissable part of the Azorean tourist itinerary, as well as imparting knowledge about the need to conserve and protect the magnificent creatures that abound in the seas around the islands.

> **A LONG AND WINDING WOAD**
>
> Thought to have been brought to the Azores by Flemish settlers, woad was cultivated in almost all of the islands until the 17th century, and was a key element in the islands' economic development through exports to the European textile centres, where it was used to produce a bright blue colour.
>
> The plant was usually sown in February, and the leaves gathered from May to September, and crushed while still green. The resultant pulp was dried in the sun, crushed again and fermented. The end product was a paste, formed into balls for ease of transportation.

Left: *Whale watching trips are an important part of the Azorean economy, and guaranteed to find something to see – or it's your money back!*

A SHOT TO NOTHING

During World War II, the Allies had entered Africa to engage Rommel's forces. Anti-aircraft batteries had been placed on São Miguel to defend against German attacks. Unfortunately, on New Year's Day, 1944, the guns opened fire on an air-plane that was taking General Eisenhower, Supreme Commander of the Allied Forces, and future President of the United States of America, back home. They missed…

From the beginning, Azoreans hunted whales for oil, and they were so successful that every major Atlantic whaling expedition would stop in the Azores. In 1979, Portugal not only outlawed whaling, but also made the deep waters around the Azores a Natural Reserve. The economic impact to the whaling industry was replaced by the eco-tourism of whale- and marine-life watching, with former whalers becoming guides, spotters, and hosts in museums.

Sperm whales, the most numerous and among the largest whales in the Azorean waters, are often seen in groups all year round, and between April and October their number increases with the arrival of whales from fur-ther south. Between February and June there is also the possibility of seeing blue whales, fin whales, humpback whales, sei whales and killer whales (orca). Dolphins sighted regularly are common Atlantic, bottlenose, Risso, Atlantic spotted and striped.

Rarely do you fail to see anything, and the experience is one of the most memorable of a visit to these islands. Everyone should go whale watching.

THE WEST
Sete Cidades ★★★

Simply breathtaking! Your first view of the Sete Cidades crater may have you wondering what all the fuss is about. And then you begin to take in the enormity of it all, the distant walls of this extinct volcanic crater, the bright, bustling town at the heart of the depression, and the richly hued lakes. The crater has a circumference of 12km (7 miles), and you can spend the best part of a day walking around the rim. The crater was formed by the consecutive collapse of two hills that surrounded it, making this one of the largest subsidence *caldeiras* in the Azores. On the steep slopes that surround it you can find traces of primi-tive vegetation, and this is also a critical area for endemic flora like the juniper, angelica, holly, heather and blue-berry. The area is also important for bird life, including some endangered species; among the endemic species are the woodpigeon of the Azores and the goldcrest.

The best view of the crater is from **Vista do Rei** (named after the visit of King Carlos I in 1901), to the south of the crater, and from here you can see the distinct difference in colouration of the lakes: one decidedly blue, the other green. Folklore tells a story of a princess who fell in love with a shepherd. For years they kept their love for one another a secret, but then the day came when the lowly shepherd asked her father for her hand in marriage. The king, rather predictably, felt that the shepherd could not maintain his princess daughter in a fitting manner, and declined. The hapless couple left it another year before once again approaching the king. The result was just the same, and, anticipating that the king would never consent to their marriage, they walked out into the heart of the crater, onto a low ridge of land. There they wept and consoled one another; the shepherd, with green eyes, wept tears that created the green lake; the princess, whose eyes were blue, wept tears to make the much larger blue lake. Cynical taxi drivers might jokingly suggest that since the blue lake is much larger than the green lake, this story demonstrates that women cry more than men!

Whatever the story, the scenery in **Sete Cidades** is both dramatic and inspirational; large green pastures dotted with cows are confined between stands of pine and Japanese cedar. The parish contains traditional houses, some with high barns. **São Nicolau church** is in neo-Gothic style, built

SETE CIDADES
Legend recounts the arrival here of seven bishops, fleeing from Portugal on the arrival of the Moors. Here, among the 'undiscovered islands', they took refuge and founded the seven cities of Sete Cidades.
Another spin on this creationist storyline says that Sete Cidades has its origin in the sequence of seven craters, resulting from volcanic eruptions that produced the seven lakes: Verde, Azul, Rasa, Santiago, Caldeiras, Secas and Alferes.

Below: *The size of the craters of Sete Cidades is immense; here there are craters within craters.*

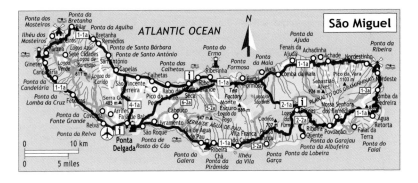

in 1852. At the end of one of the lagoons is a **tunnel**, carved through the mountains and used ostensibly as an overflow outlet for the lagoon, but which was originally used by the people of Sete Cidades as a shortcut to the 'outside world'. It takes a while to comprehend it all.

Mosteiros **

With its deep bay, Mosteiros is a prime tourist attraction, especially popular with those in search of peace and quiet. There is notable beauty here, along the flat coastal strip, called a '*fajã*', and among the four small islets, and natural swimming pools created within the basalt rocks that complement the dark sandy beach.

THE EAST

The eastern part of the island is mountainous and heavily afforested, and it has a strikingly beautiful coastline best observed, like the valleys and gorges passed en route, from one of the many *miradouros* (viewpoints) along the way. It is always worth stopping at the viewpoints; they are not placed haphazardly, and tend to give outstanding views of the landscape and coastal cliffs.

Achada das Furnas ***

The **Achada valley** is enchanting, an idyllic site grafted into the green hills and mountains. The best view of the valley is from the *miradouros* of Pico do Ferro and Salto do Cavalo further to the east. The name Furnas means 'cave',

CALDEIRAS

These bubbling, sulphurous hot 'springs' and vapours boil at around 100°C (212°F); known as *caldeiras*, they dot the landscape of Furnas providing direct and inhospitable links with the subterranean depths of the island. Around them, the air is heavy with the smell of sulphur, and those outlets of water that are safe to drink carry a distinct bitterness associated with the metallic properties of the rocks through which the water has travelled. Take care to drink, very moderately, from only those water spouts marked as safe to drink. If in doubt, head to the nearest bar and order a beer (*cerveja*).

and derives from the numerous hollows and vents in the ground from which bubble hot springs and sulphurous mud geysers overhung by plumes of steam (fumaroles). Local entrepreneurs are renowned for dropping bags of sweet corn cobs into the bubbling water to cook, and then selling them from roadside stalls. At a higher level, along the northern shore of the **Lagoa das Furnas**, the hotels bury lunch, in large pots, to be slowly cooked by the hot earth in subterranean ovens (*see Cozido à portuguesa*, page 25). *Caldeiradas de peixe* (fish bouillabaisse) is another dish cooked in this natural kitchen.

This is an excellent place to relax, and go for walks; the waters are said to be beneficial in the treatment of respiratory ailments, rheumatism, and depression! An unblocking of nasal passages can be vouched for by the author, but neither his rheumatism nor the depression of having to spend many weeks working among the Azores while writing this guide was noticeably affected!

Terra Nostra Garden ★★★

The delight of lunch at the Terra Nostra Garden Hotel is one thing; the pleasure of wandering the lush botanical gardens beyond (small admission charge) is quite another,

> ### LAGOA DAS FURNAS
>
> At 1.9km² (0.7 sq miles), Lagoa das Furnas is the second largest lake on the island of São Miguel. The lake is 281m (922ft) above sea level, and almost rectangular in shape. It is 2km (1.2 miles) long and 1.6km (1 mile) wide, and 12m (40ft) deep at its maximum. The thermal springs on its banks reach temperatures of 61.5°C (143°F).

Left: *If ever proof of modest proportions was needed that the Azores are living islands, there is none better than the many fumaroles that bubble and steam, as here at Furnas on São Miguel.*

THOMAS HICKLING

Thomas Hickling was appointed Vice Consul in Ponta Delgada in 1795. Hickling was a young American businessman who moved to São Miguel in 1769, after a disagreement with his conservative father over the younger Hickling's support for the Revolution. Hickling was an energetic entrepreneur and left stories and mementos that survive to this day. One, a rock with his name carved into it and the date '1770', is situated near one of the volcanic pools in Furnas; another a summer palace in Furnas that he called 'Yankee Hall', and which became the foundation of the renowned botanical gardens of the Art Deco Terra Nostra Hotel. He also constructed the first US Consulate building in Ponta Delgada, now the Hotel São Pedro, a hospitality school and hotel.

and likely to take up the rest of the day.

Terra Nostra Garden dates from 1780, and marks the place where Thomas Hickling, then US Consul in São Miguel, had his summer residence. The modest 2ha (5-acre) garden of Hickling later grew hugely under subsequent owners, and now provides one of the most sumptuous gardens in the Azores. Within the garden there is a section dedicated to the 56 endemic plants of the Azores, although many are typical of Macronesia, an area that also embraces Madeira, the Canary Islands and the Cape Verde archipelagos.

Close by the hotel, and in front of the Park House, is a large and very popular **thermal swimming pool**, in spite of the ferrous-coloured water that seems initially off-putting.

Elsewhere within the garden is an outstanding **azalea** collection and another section containing **cycads** from all over the world, notably Africa, South America, Asia and Australia.

Lagoa do Fogo **

'Fire Lake' is named after the 16th-century eruption that formed the crater in which the lake now sits. Clear water covers the crater floor, and a white sand beach faces across the lake to steep, vegetated cliffs. This is a hugely

Right: Yams are a popular and nutritious addition to the Azorean cuisine, and grow readily in the warm climate; here they are flourishing in the gardens of the Terra Nostra Hotel.

peaceful spot, and perfect for a day out with a picnic. This is the principal crater of Serra de Água de Pau, and the surrounding area contains vegetation of great botanical interest and was designated a Natural Reserve in 1974.

THE SOUTHEAST

Lagoa *

The streets of the small village of Lagoa are fascinating to explore. The town's harbour was used for centuries to export wheat and woad. In the 15th century, long before the Azores were fully colonized, Portuguese sailors left sheep to graze on the eastern end of the uninhabited São Miguel Island. When they returned, they found the sheep had been breeding prodigiously by a tranquil bay from then on known as Porto Dos Corneiros (The Port of the Sheep). In time this became the fishing port of Lagoa.

Today, Lagoa's natural swimming pools and beach are a popular tourist attraction, away from the bustle of Ponta Delgada. The façade of the **Cerâmica Vieira** (Rua das Alminhas 10-12, 9560 Lagoa, tel: 296 912 116) to the west of the town centre is a reminder that Lagoa is a major producer of ceramics, and the factory has an interesting **museum** of tools and artefacts. The **Church of Nossa Senhora do Rosário** is built in typically Azorean style in contrasting black-and-white stonework.

Vila Franca do Campo **

Vila Franca do Campo was the first capital of São Miguel and is currently one of the principal tourist centres of the Azorean archipelago.

The town was formed prior to 1472, and until 1499 the power of the village extended across the entire island. In this prosperous village-port resided the area's governor, landed nobles, well-to-do farmers and businessmen.

At the beginning of the 16th century, Vila Franca was São Miguel's most vital commercial port. It was also in this affluent 500-year-old village that the Governor's Palace, a beautiful temple dedicated to Saint Michael the Archangel, a chapel, and convent dedicated to Saint Francis were erected. However, the earthquake of 22 October 1522

A FRUITY STORY

Brought from South America in the 19th century, originally as an ornamental plant, the pineapple was soon found to be a viable alternative to the orange crop, at the time in a state of decline. Today, pineapples are cultivated in large greenhouses, each illustrating a stage in the 18–24-month cycle of fruit production. The greatest concentration of greenhouses is around Lagoa, Vila Franca do Campo and Fajã de Baixo north of Ponta Delgada. So successful have the pineapples of the Azores become that they have a certification of authenticity: 'Ananás dos Açores, São Miguel'.

Above: *Looking down on Vila Franca do Campo and the pineapple houses.*

destroyed and buried the village. Only by the efforts of the survivors was Vila Franca rebuilt and eventually extended to the west.

During the ensuing centuries, the local people introduced and developed many different agricultural crops, including sweet potatoes (16th century), corn (17th century), oranges and pineapples (in greenhouses) for export (19–20th century), grapes, bananas and cattle (20th century). Today, the town is also renowned for the work of its artisans, who produce fine **pottery** in dark clay.

In the town centre is a lovely square with a public garden dominated by the Gothic **Igreja do São Miguel**. On a rise above the town stands the **Ermida (Chapel) of Nossa Senhora da Paz**, approached by a long flight of steps separated by small terraces with scenes from the bible depicted in tiles on the retaining walls. From the chapel doorway there is a fine view southwards over the town, around which are rows of greenhouses growing pineapples (pointed roofs) and other vegetables, like cucumber (domed roofs).

The **Ilhéu da Vila Franca** is the crater of an ancient sunken volcano, and today classified as a Nature Reserve. The island is almost circular in shape, with a narrow ingress from the sea. The beautiful interior provides a natural swimming pool of crystal clear water. There is a regular boat service from Vila Franca do Campo from June to September.

Ribeira Quente ★
South of Furnas, the road linking to Ribeira Quente is very appealing, and well furnished with picnic and barbecue sites. The village itself – the name means 'Hot River' – is renowned for its beach warmed by hot springs.

Povoação *

Located on the south coast of the island, east of Ponta Delgada and Vila Franca do Campo, **Povoação** is linked with a road connecting Ponta Delgada and Lagoa, Furnas, and Nordeste along with the eastern part of the island and the mountain road linking to Ribeira Grande. Most of the mountains to the north of the village are covered with forests and valleys which feature creeks and streams and are generally grassy. The rest of the land is made up of agricultural meadows and forest. The highest mountains are to the northeast. The main sources of industry are agriculture and fishing.

Povoação was the area first settled after the discovery of the island. Of special interest are the oldest chapel on the island, the 'Santa Bárbara' **chapel**, which dates from the 15th century, along with the 'Matriz Velha' church, constructed on the ocean side next to the beach where the first settlers of São Miguel disembarked: both are important components of the architectural heritage of Povoação.

Nordeste *

This municipality is about as far as you can get from Ponta Delgada, and is one of the most attractive in São Miguel. Entering the town you see the gracious **Ponte de Sete Arcos** (the bridge of the seven arches), one of the largest and most beautiful bridges on the island and constructed in 1882. In the town centre, the **Igreja de São Jorge** (St George's Church), constructed during the 15th century, is worthy of mention. The **Museu do Nordeste** has an interesting ethnographic collection on working the land and sea.

Pico da Vara **

The highest point on the island, at an altitude of 1105m (3625ft), is a two-hour walk along a path offering magnificent scenery and intimate contact with nature at its most primitive (note: Pico da Vara is a Natural Reserve, and so previous authorization is required from the Regional Forestry Ministry – see page 43). The mountainous area around Pico da Vara is dissected by deep river ravines. In 1988, Pico da Vara, an area of remarkable botanical and landscape interest, was classified Partial Forest Nature

---

A SHORT-LIVED BIT OF THE BRITISH EMPIRE

On 14 June 1811, a volcanic eruption took place just off the coast of São Miguel, between Ponta da Ferraria and Ponta do Escalvado, producing a small island to a height of 70m (230ft). The English frigate *Sabrina* was in the Azorean waters at the time, and the enterprising captain took possession of the island on 4 July, and raised the British flag. Alas, seven months later, the island had slipped back beneath the waves, making the island, probably, the most short-lived of British territories.

**RIBEIRA GRANDE
GEOTHERMAL PLANT**

Research into the use of deep
waters heated by magma began
in 1978, to a depth of 1200m
(3900ft), and this permitted the
installation of an electricity-
generating turbine using steam
from the underground water.
The success of this enterprise
led to the construction of two
geothermal plants, thereby
reducing the island's dependency on fossil fuels.

Reserve, and it is also part of the Natura 2000 network,
classified as a Special Protection Area (SPA).

Pico da Vara is predominantly covered in dense **laurel**
forest, which links back to the humid forests of the
Tertiary Period. These forests existed in southern Europe,
but largely disappeared millions of years ago during the
last glacial period.

THE NORTH COAST ★★★

Overall, the area is characterized by an irregular landscape almost entirely covered with trees. Many of the
exotic sylvan species used for the production of wood and
for the protection of properties, along with a great variety
of other lush vegetation, are abundant here. The **viewpoints**, Ponta da Madrugada, Ponta do Sossego, Salto da
Farinha, and the Ponta do Estorninho, are all worth visiting
to admire the incredible coastal landscape.

Ribeira Grande ★★

The north coastal town of **Ribeira Grande** derives its name
from the river flowing through it from Lagoa do Fogo (*see*
page 36). The first settlers set up water mills here for grain,
and later for use in the production of woad for dyeing.
Milling was one of the economic mainstays of the town's
economy until the mid-20th century. Today, Ribeira

Below: *Ribeira Grande,
Igreja da Nossa Senhora
da Estrela.*

Grande is the second largest town on São Miguel in terms of population, and was granted city status in 1981.

Although largely dominated by **religious architecture** – Nossa Senhora da Estrela, Espírito Santo (Holy Spirit), Nossa Senhora da Conceição (Our Lady of Conception), and Igreja e Convento de São Francisco (Church and Convent of Saint Francis) – the town has considerable interest, and the churches, key to the Azorean way of life, are the principal locations for religious gatherings. In particular, the **Igreja de Nossa Senhora da Estrela** has a remarkable glass showcase with very small figurines moulded from bread dough, Arabic paste and albumen. The remains of a fountain are visible below ground level, one of the few vestiges of the 16th-century town.

The **City Hall** and the **Ethnographic Museum** house traditional works in stone (basalt), and are typical examples of Azorean architecture from the 16th and 17th centuries. Various **chapels** dedicated to saints are valuable examples of Baroque architecture. In addition, the older manors found here and in the surrounding villages are of note.

A short distance from Ribeira Grande is the **Caldeiras da Ribeira Grande**, an area where bubbling fumaroles are found encompassed by a lush grove of trees.

The **Caldeira Velha** is especially delightful, and worth tracing the winding roads to find. Here you walk through what elsewhere in the world would be a subtropical rainforest with huge ferns, palms and a rash of ginger lilies to reach, first, a bubbling muddy fumarole. A little way further you arrive at a pool at the base of a small waterfall; the warm water makes this a popular place for a quick dip.

A little further up the valley is **Lombadas**, the site of the naturally carbonated spring that provides the mineral water known as **Água das Lombadas**.

Above: *This waterfall at the Caldeira Velha feeds warm water into a small pool that is popular with bathers.*

São Miguel at a Glance

As with all the islands, São Miguel can be visited year round, but **Jul** and **Aug** are the most popular months. Anyone not restricted to holidays during these months should consider visiting at other times of year; not all facilities will be up to speed, but **spring** is an especially attractive time as the flowers come into bloom, and the months from Apr to Oct are when you are most likely to appreciate the whale watching opportunity. The island enjoys a temperate, maritime climate with comfortable temperatures that rarely reach freezing at coast level, and only produce a frost above 1000m (3280ft). In **summer**, the temperature can rise to 27°C (81°F), but seldom higher. There is **rainfall** in every month, but for the most part it is not long lasting. **Humidity** is usually within a narrow range, 80–85%, but can increase to 100%.

From the UK between Apr and Oct there are flights direct from London Gatwick to Ponta Delgada on São Miguel on Tuesdays and Saturdays. **From Dublin** there is one flight per week on Fridays between May and Sep. These flights are operated by SATA Internacional (www.sata.pt), who also fly direct from other European cities: Lisbon and Porto (Portugal), Funchal (Madeira), Frankfurt

(Germany), Amsterdam (Netherlands), and Paris (France), and via Lisbon from a wider range of cities.
The Portuguese airline (TAP) has flights from London Heathrow or Gatwick via Lisbon to Ponta Delgada (www.flytap.com). SAS Airlines, the Scandinavian airline, has flights to Ponta Delgada from Oslo.

Local buses tend to operate mainly in response to the needs of local people, not tourists, making this an interesting but unreliable option. One of the best ways of getting around, especially if you have limited time, is to hire a taxi for a day or half-day tour. Ask your hotel to find an English-speaking driver, but try to book a day or so ahead, as they are popular during the main season. Taxi rates on São Miguel are fixed (ranging in 2007 from €55 to €155 for up to four passengers, depending on the tour), and most hotels have leaflets explaining the different tours that are available, and the rates. Elsewhere, it is a matter of negotiation.

There are **hotels** of all standards on São Miguel. There are, at the time of writing, no five-star hotels, although one seems imminent in Ponta Delgada. But reliance on a star rating can be misleading: the

four-star Holiday Inn in Ponta Delgada (see below), for example, is modern, bright, spacious and friendly, but its 'Kids go free' policy, allowing children under 18 to share their parents' room, makes this an ideal proposition for those on a budget.
Holiday Inn, Avenue D. João III 29, 9500-310 Ponta Delgada, São Miguel, tel: 296 630 000. Impressive modern hotel on a hill overlooking Ponta Delgada. Huge rooms, swimming pool, gymnasium, Jacuzzi, pool table, bar, restaurant, souvenir shop. Outside the main tourist season the evening meal is a buffet; lunch, however, remains as à la carte.
Terra Nostra Garden Hotel, Rue Padre José Jacinto Botelho, 9675-061 Furnas, São Miguel, tel: 296 549 090. Three-star hotel, yet very luxurious because of the fabulous 12ha (30-acre) gardens to which hotel guests are admitted free. Panoramic restaurant, bar, gym, indoor and outdoor swimming pools. Well away from the bustle of Ponta Delgada, and possibly the best place to enjoy cozido.
Hotel do Colégio, Rua Carvalho Araújo 39, 9500-040 Ponta Delgada, São Miguel, tel: 296 306 600. In a side street, this hotel is a real find, and has an excellent restaurant (A Colmeia), 55 rooms, health centre, exterior heated swimming pool, gymnasium and Turkish bath.

Caloura Hotel Resort, 9560-260 Água de Pau, tel: 296 960 900, fax: 296 960 909, www.calourahotel.com Midway between Lagoa and Vila Franca da Campo, this modern hotel overlooks the sea. It has 80 fully equipped rooms with cable TV, bar, excellent restaurant (Barrocas do Mar), swimming pool. Runs diving and scuba diving programmes.

WHERE TO EAT

There is no excuse for not dining well in São Miguel. There are many small bar-restaurants in Ponta Delgada, and even a few Chinese restaurants. But keep an eye open for restaurants dotted further afield around the island; many have excellent menus and wine lists.
A Colmeia Restaurant, Travessa do Colégio, 9500-040 Ponta Delgada, tel: 296 306 600. In the Hotel do Colégio, this is a stylish restaurant serving traditional cuisine cooked to the highest standards, supported by an excellent array of Portuguese wines. This is the only restaurant where there is a separate menu offering dishes that use island-produced and certificated beef. Don't make plans for the rest of the evening. Just relax.
O Corisco Bar-Restaurant, Rua Manuel da Ponte 28, 9500-085 Ponta Delgada, tel: 296 284 444. Don't give up trying to find this place; persevere, you won't be disappointed. It's not

far from the city gates, and is exactly the place to go for typically Azorean cuisine.
Borda d'Água Restaurant, Largo do Porto 52, Rosário, 9560 Lagoa, tel/fax: 296 912 114. The place to go for the freshest fish in all the Azores. Reserving a table is a good idea. Outdoor terrace, and plenty of room inside. No credit cards accepted.
Montemira, Canada da Fita 28, Santa Cruz, 9560-031 Lagoa, tel/fax: 296 916 034. A modern, stylish restaurant. The talented and imaginative chef produces interesting food combinations and excellent steak – try the Montemira Steak.
Churrasqueira Café Snack Bar, Estrada Regional 107, 9545-218 Fenais da Luz, tel: 296 919 474. You'll drive past this a hundred times and not see it. Here they really keep it simple, which is ideal if you are exploring with a family in tow. Don't ask for the menu, there isn't one.

TOURS AND EXCURSIONS

Whale Watching Tours
There are many companies offering tours on most of the islands. Some of the 'Round the Island' tour operators offer whale watching and diving tours also. Here are just a few:
Futurismo, Marina Pêro de Teive, 9500 Ponta Delgada, tel: 296 628 522, www.azoreswhales.com
Sea Watch Açores, Avenue Infante Dom Henrique, 9500

Ponta Delgada, tel: 296 584 670, www.seawatch.com.pt
Round the Island Tours
Offering a range of possibilities, the following companies arrange half-day and day-long tours around the island. They can all arrange hotel pick-ups:
AVA Guided Tours, tel: 296 305 130, www.avatours.com
Melo Travel, Rua de Santa Luzia 7-11, 9500-114 Ponta Delgada, tel: 296 205 385.
Panazorica Tours, tel: 296 301 723, www.panazorica.com
Flight Sightseeing
Take an aerial view of the island. **Aero Clube de São Miguel**, Nordela, 9600-674 Ponta Delgada, tel: 296 284 771.

USEFUL CONTACTS

Tourist Offices
Delegação de Turismo de São Miguel, Avenue Infante Dom Henrique, 9500-150 Ponta Delgada, tel: 296 285 743 or 296 285 152, fax: 296 282 211, email: info.turismo@drt.raa.pt
Tourist Information Desks
Airport: Aeroporto João Paulo II, 9500 Ponta Delgada, tel: 296 284 569.
Furnas: Rua Frederico Moniz Pereira 14, 9675 Furnas, tel/fax: 296 584 525.
Regional Forestry Ministry
Direcção Regional dos Recursos Florestais, Rua do Contador 23, 9500-050 Ponta Delgada, tel: 296 286 288, email: info.drrf@azores.gov.pt www.azores.gov.pt

3
Santa Maria

The eastern islands are just two in number: São Miguel and the much smaller Santa Maria. São Miguel is 'where it's at', the main centre for the whole of the islands; Santa Maria, no less endearing, is quite at the other end of the scale, and most certainly a place for those who like to wander peaceably among fine scenery with the sea never far away. It is not possible to have two such markedly contrasting islands.

The island of Santa Maria is the most southerly of the Azores, the nearest to mainland Portugal, and said to be the first to have been discovered (in 1427), although this is still debated by historians and some records suggest that it was a friar, Frei Gonçalo Velho Cabral, who discovered the island in 1432. It was certainly the first to hear the news that there was land beyond the western horizon when Columbus is believed to have stopped off here in 1492, returning from the Indies. Santa Maria was also the first island of the Azores to be settled when, in 1439, a small group of pioneers landed at Praia do Lobos ('the beach of the wolves', not that there were ever any wolves here; *lobos* was the name given to sea lions), on the banks of a stream called the Ribeira do Capitão (now the Ribeira de Santana). Settlement then took on a pace, increasing rapidly during the rest of the century with the result that the place called Porto, later renamed Vila do Porto, was the first Azorean town to receive a charter.

Geologically, Santa Maria is the only island in the Azores to have fossil-bearing rocks of sedimentary origin in the form of limestone from towards the end of the

Don't Miss

** **Vila do Porto:** the island's principal town stretches along a basalt plateau between two ravines.
** **Baía de São Lourenço:** once a crater, long since filled by the sea.
* **Anjos:** this tiny village can boast a most ancient chapel.
* **Maia:** a small coastal village, sandwiched between cliffs and the sea.
* **Santo Espírito:** visit the Cooperativa de Artesanato de Santa Maria to buy locally produced handicrafts.

Opposite: *The doorway where Columbus attended Mass, Anjos.*

VITAL STATISTICS

Santa Maria is about 88km
(55 miles) from São Miguel
(25 minutes by plane), and
the third smallest island of
the Azores. The surface area is
approximately 97km² (37 sq
miles). The island has 5550
inhabitants (2007), and the
municipal seat is located in
Vila do Porto.

Miocene period (about 5 million BP). The original island
rose above the sea at this time, and then sank back again
allowing further sedimentation to occur.

The interior landscape of Santa Maria is varied, with a
hilly region in the northeast around Santa Bárbara and
Santo Espírito, and a more level region to the southwest
around Vila do Porto. There is quite a contrast between
the two halves, east and west, of the island. Where the airport is, in the west, the landscape is barren. But progress
towards the hilly areas in the east and the change is rapid,
becoming the typical Azorean scene of lush pastures,
Japanese cedar, wild flowers and native shrubs. The whole
coastline is indented, with headlands and inlets, and
numerous white, sandy beaches.

First impressions of Santa Maria, particularly if you arrive

on a day when sea mist is shroud-
ing the island, may seem a little
off-putting. Moreover, the somewhat drier climate produces a
parchment of yellow grass, which
earned the island the name, the
'Yellow Island'. The original prosperity of the island came from the
cultivation of woad, much the
same as São Miguel.

Santa Maria is one of the most
pleasant islands, with an agreeable climate, plenty of beaches,
and a rural landscape that is dotted with white-painted houses. It
is a little underdeveloped touristi-
cally, but a delightful place to
relax and slow down. The way to
get the best from Santa Maria is to
hire a car or a taxi, and tour the
island's meandering roads, stopping off at some secluded beach –
the white sand is quite unusual
among the Azores – or maybe for
a picnic. This is not a place where

Left: *Rooftop detail, Vila do Porto, Santa Maria.* **Opposite:** *Monument commemorating the discovery of Santa Maria.*

haste has any worthwhile meaning; Santa Maria is for taking it easy, a place to recharge the batteries. Increasingly, however, water-sports enthusiasts are visiting Santa Maria and the beaches are a marked contrast with the varied landscape of the interior. There is an effort being made to encourage walkers, too, and there is plenty of excellent walking to be enjoyed, but at present little of it is waymarked, although some new waymark signposts are gradually appearing. *See* 'Travel Tips' (page 126) for a recommended book on walking in the Azores.

VILA DO PORTO ★★

The island's principal town stretches along a basalt plateau between two ravines. It is a relaxing town and its main buildings, dating from the 16th and 17th centuries, are the **Convento de Santo António**, now seeing service as the public library, and the Franciscan monastery, currently the **Town Hall**. Other places of interest in the town are the **Fort of São Brás**, built in the 16th century to defend the town at a time when Portugal was under Spanish rule.

PRAIA FORMOSA ★

This village is located in one of the loveliest corners of the island, and has a fine sandy beach, arguably the best on the island. It has a growing reputation, too, as a good place for surfing, sailing, water-skiing and swimming. It lies just below the village of **Almagreira**, a place itself endowed

---

A TASTE OF SANTA MARIA

Santa Maria Island turnip broth (*Caldo de nabos*): The broth used to boil turnips is also used to cook the remaining vegetables and pork meat. The broth is then poured over bread slices, and served as a rich soup or with the meat and vegetables separately. It was said in writings dated 1577 that 'the vegetables of this island are the best', but the Santa Maria turnip is not a turnip, nor a beetroot, nor a cabbage, but something that has the characteristics of all three.

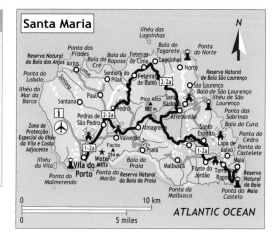

with charm. The village name derives from *almagre*, signifying a deep red soil used to glaze pottery. In the garden of a house in **Covas** are some of the *mata-mouras*, or small hollows dug into the ground, then topped with a basalt lug and used to conceal grain from pirates.

PICO ALTO ★★

Not surprisingly, the panorama from the highest point of the island (587m/1925ft) takes in the whole island, and the spread of deep valleys, the indented coastline, and the lush, colourful vegetation. The area around the mountain is an especially good place to see specimens of the island's original vegetation – heather, laurel, juniper and Scottish heather. It is possible to drive almost to the top of the mountain.

Baía do São Lourenço ★★

Once a crater, long since filled by the sea, the Baía do São Lourenço is a beautiful sight with concave slopes terraced by vineyards corralled into neat plots bounded by basalt rock walls. The grapes are used to make wine, but not usually for resale, just local consumption. There is fine scenery here, a white sand beach and natural swimming pools where you can sea-bathe without the inherent risk of being swept away.

SANTO ESPÍRITO ★

This is the most important village in the southeastern part of the island, and possesses an attractive church – **Nossa Senhora da Purificação** – boasting a beautiful Baroque façade and black basalt sculptures, the most unusual in all the Azores. Built in the 16th century and modified in the 18th century, this church is one of the most harmonious structures of the island and, according to legend, stands on the site where the first Holy Spirit Mass was celebrated in the archipelago. Well worth visiting is the small building that houses the **Cooperativa de Artesanato de Santa Maria**, where all handicraft items on display are still made in the traditional way, and available for sale, notably bread, sweets, tapestry and weaving.

Housed in an early 20th-century house, the **Museum of Santa Maria** is simply a display of the furniture and contents of a typical house. Open May–September: Tuesday–Friday, 09:30–12:30, 14:00–17:30; weekends 14:00–17:30. October–April: Tuesday–Friday, 10:00–12:00, 14:00–17:00.

HOUSES OF SANTA MARIA

The traditional houses of Santa Maria are rectangular with projecting kitchens and round ovens, roofed in local clay tiles, and inspired by the architecture of the Algarve and Alentejo. The houses are all whitewashed, and their window and door frames highlighted in bright colours – green, blue, yellow or red – that contrast agreeably with the white of the building. Most have large cylindrical or rectangular chimneys, a distinctive style typical of the island. The houses with two floors were built by Azorean emigrants who came back from overseas. Beside most of the houses are corn stores formed by crossed poles, known as 'donkeys', on which the corn is hung out to dry.

Left: *Vernacular cottage and chimney, Santa Maria.*

Right: *The symmetrical pattern of cultivation terraces is typical of the Azorean islands, as here at Maia on Santa Maria.*

MAIA *

This small coastal village, sandwiched between cliffs and the sea, also has a natural swimming pool. The road ends at a huge waterfall, the **Foz da Ribeira Grande**, that plunges (or sometimes dribbles) down a sheer black cliff. On the way to the village, the road passes (at a distance) the **Gonçalo Velho lighthouse** perched on the high rocks of the Ponta do Castelo.

THE NORTH COAST AND BARREIRO DA FANECA *

Much of the north coast of Santa Maria is a Protected Landscape of Regional Interest, including the area of arid and clayey land called the Barreiro da Faneca, along with the Cré, Raposa and Tagarete bays and their adjacent cliffs.

The Barreiro da Faneca is a gently undulating area with minimal drainage and is a unique and colourful landscape within the whole of the Azores, known as 'The Red Desert of the Azores'. It is less colourful now than of old due to the spread of vegetation, notably heather, scabious, spurge and laurel.

Cré and **Raposa** bays display several outcrops of fossilized sediment, mainly limestone, sandstone, shales and conglomerates. Both bays are bordered by steep sea cliffs, from 50–150m (165–490ft) high, that provide nesting grounds for Cory's shearwater, and the common and roseate tern. **Tagarete Bay** has even higher cliffs, the result of the sea erosion that has shaped so much of the coastline of Santa Maria. In addition to the birds found at Cré and Raposa bays, those at Tagarete Bay also find favour with little shearwater and the Madeiran petrel, making this an 'Important Bird Area', and one of keen interest to ornithologists. Equally important for roseate tern in particular is the islet of Lagoinhas, around 300m (984ft) offshore.

ANJOS *

The tiny village of Anjos on the northern coast can boast arguably the most ancient chapel of the whole archipelago, the **Chapel of Nossa Senhora dos Anjos**. This tiny whitewashed building, restored in 1893, is the place where Christopher Columbus is believed to have stopped as he was returning from discovering the Americas and, keeping a promise made when a storm threatened his ship, ordered the celebration of Mass at the first port they put into. The pulpit inside, probably dating from the restoration of the chapel, has some intricate carving. Also within is a *retablo* that, so a tradition says, was the portable altar from the ship in which the pioneer settler, Gonçalo Velho, arrived in Santa Maria.

GATHERING LICHEN

Roccella (*Roccella lichen*) was used to make a very fine dye, and it grows in abundance in the clear air of the Azores. It was a major business for the islanders from the 15th to mid-19th centuries when it was replaced by aniline dyes. Santa Maria produced large quantities of the lichen, but gathered it at great risk as the men had to clamber up and down steep cliffs hanging on ropes. It is said that the name of a headland to the west of Ponta do Castelo – Ponta da Malbusca (meaning 'Ill-fated search') – is a reference to the dangers of this task.

Left: *Chapel of Nossa Senhora dos Anjos, Anjos, Santa Maria.*

Right: *Pulpit carving,*
Chapel of Nossa Senhora
dos Anjos, Anjos, Santa
Maria.

HANDICRAFTS

The island of Santa Maria produces a variety of handicrafts, items for everyday use made from local materials. With an abundance of clay, pottery has always been a principal craft, although the activity has significantly diminished in the last 50 years. The many sheep on the island supply the wool to manufacture handmade sweaters and rugs woven on rustic looms, along with bedspreads and linen cloth. Wickerwork also has a place on the island, mainly to produce practical objects for local use, but also items for the tourist trade.

CULINARY MATTERS

Fish and shellfish from the sea and meat from the pastured animals are the basis of the cuisine of Santa Maria. With a 'chuck it all in and see what comes out' approach to cooking, all of these ingredients are added to turnip broth, soups and stews, along with *bolo na panela* ('cake in the pan') and home-made sausages. Visitors with a sweet tooth can assault meringues (*suspiros*), honey cakes (*melindres*), sugar-coated biscuit rings (*cavacas*), and brandy biscuits (*biscoitos de aguardente*).

Whether Columbus actually anchored in Anjos is another matter. Arriving on the wings of a storm, Columbus is said to have lost an anchor, and had to cut the other two free. Historians debate whether the explorer put into safety in Anjos or in the safer Cré bay a little further to the east. However, three ancient anchors were found in Cura Bay on the eastern coast of the island, and speculation suggests these may be the anchors from Columbus' ship.

SANTANA

This tiny village is thought to be the site of the first settlement on the island, the surrounding plateau now dominated by the airport from which a track leads down to **Ponta do Malmerendo** with its small lighthouse. The so-called 'Burma Road' (*Estrada da Birmânia*), named after the American soldiers who built it to open up access to the site of the future airport, leads to the tiny port.

Santa Maria at a Glance

Santa Maria can be visited year round, although **July** and **August** are the most popular months. **Spring** is an especially attractive time as the flowers come into bloom, and the months from April to October are when you are most likely to appreciate the whale watching opportunity. The island enjoys comfortable temperatures that rarely reach freezing. In **summer**, the temperature can rise to 27°C (80°F), but seldom higher. As with all the islands there is **rainfall** in every month, but for the most part it is not long lasting. **Humidity** is usually within a narrow range, 80–85%, but can increase to 100%.

Between Santa Maria and São Miguel there are frequent flights throughout the year, at varying times, operated by **SATA Air Açores**. Flying time is around 20–25 minutes. Remarkably, for such a small island, the runway on Santa Maria can accommodate aircraft up to 747 'Jumbo' size, although no such tourist flights operate. In fact, the large size of the runway has its roots in its construction and use by American forces.

Local buses operate mainly in response to the needs of local people, not tourists, making this an interesting but unreli-

able option. There is **hire car** potential on Santa Maria, and the tourist office is at the airport. Unless intending to do little, one of the best ways of getting around, especially if time is limited and map reading not regarded as a key component of a relaxing holiday, is to hire a taxi for a day or half-day tour. Ask the hotel to find an English-speaking driver, but try to book a day or so ahead. Across the islands, taxi rates vary a little, and on Santa Maria it may be a question of an hourly rate.

Hotel Columbo, Lugar da Cruz Teixeira, 9580-473 Vila do Porto, Santa Maria, tel: 296 820 200, www.colombo-hotel.com In spite of looking a bit like a block of unimaginative government offices, and with a rather Spartan restaurant and breakfast room, the Hotel Columbo is comfortable, although it is set about a 20-minute walk from the main street of Vila do Porto. It has 100 rooms, five suites, restaurant, bar, outdoor pool.
Hotel Santa Maria, Rua do Horta, 9580-421 Aeroporto de Santa Maria, tel: 296 820 660. Forty-six rooms, restaurant and bar, built on the site of the wartime officers' mess, and with the advantage of all being on one level, and each room having access to a large garden.

Hotel Praia de Lobos, 9580-525 Vila do Porto, Santa Maria, tel: 296 882 286, fax: 296 882 482. Somewhere a little above 'Budget'. A simple, but well-located hotel on the main street, with 34 good-sized rooms, restaurant, bar and guest lounge.

This lovely island doesn't pretend to haute cuisine; everything is basic but wholesome. The à la carte menu at the **Hotel Columbus** is about as good as it gets, but much will have to change before they win awards for cooking.
O Ilhéu Snack Bar, São Lourenço, 9580 Vila do Porto, tel: 296 886 093. Simple, unpretentious, open all year (winter time weekends only), and serving some 'fast food', but a fair selection of dishes cooked on an outdoors barbecue. Deserves visiting.
Restaurant Atlantida, Rua Teóf Braga, Vila do Porto (main street), tel: 296 882 330. A surprisingly good menu offering both fish and meat, and some agreeable wines.

Tourist Information Desks
Airport, Apartado 560, 9580 Vila do Porto, tel: 296 886 355.
Santa Maria Environmental Department, tel: 296 882 100/10.
Vila do Porto City Hall, tel: 296 820 000 or 296 882 332.

4
Terceira

The Portuguese word for 'third', Terceira was indeed the third island in the Azores to be discovered, and it is the third largest, after São Miguel and Pico. Historically, settlement began in 1450 with a small colony at Porto Judeu and another at Praia da Vitória. Originally the island was named the Island of Jesus Christ, before a more mundane title was settled on.

The landscape of Terceira is less striking than some of the other islands, but it is more fascinating at a human level, especially in terms of its architecture and festivals. As with other islands, the economy revolved around farming, mainly cereals and the production of woad. Tourism is playing an increasingly important part of the economy of the island; the airport at Lajes has been completely renovated, and hotel standards are improving by the year. Moreover, Terceira is very much a hub for the other islands, with flights connecting to Graciosa, São Jorge and Faial.

Geographically, Terceira is a tableland of four overlapping stratovolcanoes built above a fissure zone, which rise from a depth of over 1500m (5000ft) on the floor of Atlantic Ocean, and overlooked in the east by **Serra do Cume**, the remains of Cinquo Picos, the oldest volcano on the island, with a *caldeira* that is 7km (4 miles) in diameter, one of the largest in the Azores. The centre-south of the island is consumed by a vast crater, Caldeira de Guilherme Moniz, which, as elsewhere, is surrounded by other evidence of volcanic activity. Just to its north is Pico Alto, probably less than 60,000 years old. It, too, once had

DON'T MISS

*** Angra do Heroísmo: city of traditional buildings (World Heritage Site).
*** Algar do Carvão: a wonderful underground experience.
** Angra do Heroísmo Museum: this is the main museum collection on the island.
** Monte Brasil: for a fine view over the island's capital.
** Alta da Memória: a spiky little memorial to the visit of King Pedro IV.
** Praia da Vitória: relax on a superb white sand beach, and explore the old village streets.

Opposite: *Biscoitos Vineyard and Wine Museum.*

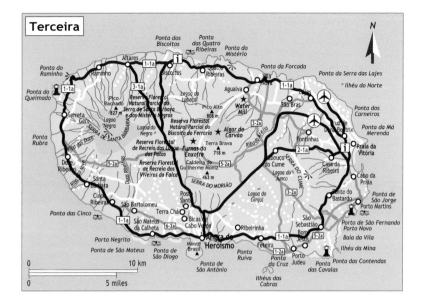

Terceira is the most densely populated island of the central group, covering an area of 382km² (147 sq miles), with a maximum length and width of 29km (18 miles) and 18km (11 miles) respectively. Terceira has a mild and most agreeable climate, an easy place to relax and enjoy good food and wine. The population in 2006 was estimated to be 55,697. Terceira Island is divided into the municipalities of **Angra do Heroísmo** and **Praia da Vitória**. Angra do Heroísmo, the historical capital of the Azores, is the oldest city in the Azores, dating back to 1534. The island has two ports – Angra do Heroísmo and Praia da Vitória – and a military base at Lajes.

a *caldeira*, but subsequent eruptions filled it with smaller lava domes and cones which top out at 808m (2651ft). In the west, **Serra de Santa Bárbara** is the island's youngest and historically active volcanic mountain (1762) and, at 1023m (3356ft), the highest.

The western part of Terceira Island is more heavily forested than the eastern part, due to the prevailing westerly winds bringing increased precipitation to that side. Most of the island is ringed by steep coastal cliffs, making access to the sea difficult except on the south coast near Angra do Heroísmo. Here, an eruption of basaltic lava in shallow water formed the tuff cone of **Monte Brasil**, which protects and shelters the harbour of the island's capital. The cone is about 1km (0.6 mile) in diameter and rises 205m (673ft) above the western side of the harbour. Elsewhere, the indented coastline is dotted with small communities, the surrounding fields divided by hedgerows and walls and used to grow produce, including grapes, for local consumption. Inland the lush green pastures contrast with rocky black terraces called **mistérios**, volcanic debris, shapely peaks, beautiful lakes and craters.

Most of the centres of population lie around the edges of the island, leaving the interior a largely treeless countryside of pastures and fields, parcelled into neat packages by basalt stone walls. But trees do exist in abundance, especially in the **Serrata Forest** to the northwest of Santa Bárbara, where eucalypts scent the air, and Japanese cedar and juniper grow in profusion.

On 1 January 1980 a violent **earthquake** shook the island and neighbouring Graciosa and São Jorge, damaging large areas and a huge amount of property. Some accounts suggest that notwithstanding the size and force of the earthquake no lives were lost, but other versions of the event suggest that as many as 50 people died, and many thousands were made homeless, which is a more likely scenario. All around the island of Terceira you encounter derelict properties from this time, although most property has now been restored.

A TASTE OF TERCEIRA

Rump steak: The first cattle were brought to Terceira in 1451; not surprisingly, steak features on many menus. Marinated in wine, with a hint of spices, then it is placed in an oven and cooked slowly for hours. Allow to cool, and then re-heat before serving. Perfect!

Left: *The north coast cliffs of Terceira, here near Biscoitos are both dramatic and permanently on the brink of collapse.*

NATURAL SWIMMING POOLS

The volcanic nature of Terceira, with lava spilling down to the sea, has created numerous areas that, in effect, have become natural swimming pools. In quite a few places, the local authorities have helped things along by constructing walkways between the pools and installing handrails to make getting in and out easier. With such clean water around the island, these natural swimming pools, constantly washed by the sea, are hugely popular, especially on sunny days, and a delight to dive into.

Of dubious notoriety, it was on 16 March 2003 that the US President and the Prime Ministers of the UK, Spain and Portugal met on Terceira to discuss the invasion of Iraq, which began four days later.

ANGRA DO HEROÍSMO ★★★

The city of Angra do Heroísmo lies along the south coast of Terceira, set in the curve of a wide bay, or *angra*. They say that to visit Angra do Heroísmo is to wander through the pages of a story that is centuries old, yet with an influence on today's world: a voyage in time that helps your discovery of just how much unites humanity.

The first settlers recognized the advantage of the ring of hills ranged behind today's city. One location, known simply as the creek, or 'angra' in Portuguese, had what was needed to construct a port where men-of-war and caravels could anchor – deep waters protected on most sides. The first houses were built along steep and winding streets on the hills, and a defensive castle built on the peak of **Outeiro**, where today a **monument** stands.

Angra is the headquarters of a military command, and the residence of a Roman Catholic bishop. Regarded by

Left: *The twin domes of Monte Brasil are a spectacular location and a nature reserve, but one that offers a fine view over the city of Angra do Heroísmo.*

many as the most beautiful town in the Azores, its principal buildings are the cathedral, military college, arsenal and observatory. The buildings are of particular interest, being a fusion of styles and features from Portugal, Brazil, England and even America. The town is laid out in a defensive pattern, given its position as a key stopping-off place on the transatlantic routes of the 16th and 17th centuries. The harbour is now of little commercial importance, but was formerly a key naval station, sheltered on the west and southwest by the promontory of Monte Brasil. Today, Angra's harbour is inferior to the neighbouring ports of Ponta Delgada (São Miguel) and Horta (Faial). Foreign trade is not large, consisting chiefly of the exportation of pineapples and other fruit.

To the west of the city, the twin domes of **Monte Brasil** are a spectacular location and a nature reserve, but one that offers some of the finest views of Terceira. To benefit fully, ascend to the **Pico das Cruzinhas**, the highest point (205m/673ft), to get the full **panorama** and see into the crater, now overgrown with scrub and used by the military as a firing range from time to time. On the way you encounter said military as you pass around the **Castle of São João Baptista**, one of the most imposing Portuguese fortresses from the 16th century, built on the orders of Philip II of Spain at the foot of Monte Brasil. The main

> ### WORLD HERITAGE SITE
>
> In 1983, the historical centre of Angra do Heroísmo was classified by UNESCO as a **World Heritage Site**. This evocative area lies beyond the Baia de Angra, where once galleons tied up, amid a network of streets built on a geometric pattern. Within an area bordered by the harbour, Rua Direita, Rua da Sé and Rua Gonçalo Velho, many of the buildings have the wrought-iron balconies with brightly painted façades typical of the Azores. UNESCO's decision to classify the central zone of the town as a World Heritage Site reflects its unparalleled position in history. The site covers an area of around 6km² (2 sq miles), half of which is made up of a major portion of the old city, and the other the extinct volcano of Monte Brasil.

Right: *The fort of São
João Baptista sits at the
foot of Monte Brasil:
within the fort, the Igreja
de São João Baptista was
built to commemorate the
restoration of Portuguese
sovereignty in 1640.*

doorway is carved in black stone, and forms part of one
of the largest examples of military architecture in Europe
from this time. Inside the fort is a church, the **Igreja de
São João Baptista**, built to commemorate the restoration
of Portuguese sovereignty in 1640. The public can join
guided tours of the fortress. Ask at the tourist office for
information about visits: in summer there is usually a
guided tour on the hour, but it is wise to ask before walking up to the entrance.

The summit of Monte Brasil is adorned by a tall stone
cross and British gun emplacements from World War II.

MOO-TORWAY MADNESS

During 2007, beside the main
highway linking Angra do
Heroísmo and Praia da Vitória,
work began on the construction of parallel roads to help
alleviate the incidence of death
by bovine encounter that
occurs along the highway, by
building new roads alongside
the *via rapida* just for cows and
farm vehicles.

The Cathedral (Sé) ★

Built in the 16th century on the site of a 15th-century
Gothic church, the interior is especially interesting, with
carved cedar wood ceiling and jacaranda furniture. The
cathedral is the Episcopal See of the Azores, and was dam-
aged, as was much else, during the 1980 earthquake.

Palácio dos Capitães-Generais (Palace of the Captains-General') ★

The palace became the residence of the Captains-General
in 1776, and has accumulated a fine collection of furni-

ture, tapestries and other works of art, including one room that contains life-size portraits of all the kings of the House of Bragança up to the reign of Queen Maria II.

Paços do Concelho (The Town Hall) *

At the heart of the city, the town hall is an impressive building constructed in the 19th century on the site of a similar structure from two centuries earlier.

Angra do Heroísmo Museum **

This is the main museum collection on the island, housed in an old convent. Its permanent and temporary collections give an interesting and broad overview of the history of the city and the island, notably the discovery of the islands, the city of Angra do Heroísmo, the relationship between the Azores and the rest of the world, as well as paintings on wood dating from the 16th and 17th centuries. The building is architecturally important, once the headquarters of a Franciscan order. The adjacent **church**, built during the 18th century, houses a fine collection of **glazed tiles**. It was here that the brother of Vasco da Gama was buried after he died while returning from India in 1499.

Alta da Memória **

This spiky little character, an obelisk, serves as a memorial to the visit of King Pedro IV, and is built on the site of the

Left: *Ornate wrought-iron balconies are an architectural detail that is commonplace across all the islands of the Azores.*

A LOAD OF BULL

Drive across the centre of the island and you encounter numerous pastures in which young, fit and healthy black bulls look ready to menace; they are one of the reasons why footpaths for walking have not developed extensively. But the bulls are destined for one of the arenas in which, during the summer months, more than 200 bullfights (*tourada*) take place, many in the new bull-ring at Angra do Heroísmo – the old bullring is now a sports centre. Unlike in Spain, the bulls used in the Azores are not fatally injured; it is the young men who take them on who are at risk. Marginally less dangerous, and of particular relevance to Terceira, are the famous *touradas à corda*, which involve a bull held on a rope by four men who allow the beast to rush at the crowds of men in the village streets, who hasten away leaving the bravest (or the least nimble) to taunt the bull by opening an umbrella under its nose.

town's first castle. Only go to see it if you want to experience the view: you need to walk through the municipal garden and take a stepped path at the back, following this upwards via many, many steps until finally you reach the large plinth on which the memorial stands. There is a fine view back over Angra do Heroísmo to Monte Brasil in particular, and this is a good place to come to pick out the various buildings and features of the town. It is a bit of a hike, but one that is worth the effort: take it easy and rest on the way up.

Museu Vulcano-Espeleológio ★

The place to go if you want to understand what you are standing on. The museum, dedicated to vulcanism, contains the largest collection in the Azores of geological samples.

Bettencourt Palace ★

This Baroque building dates from the late 17th to early 18th centuries, and is a typical example of Angra's mansion houses. Many of the rooms have ceilings and wall panels made from Brazilian and local cedar, and the main façade has an attractive portico carved from regional stone.

Porto Martins ★

This is a quiet resort of mainly summer residences owned by wealthy islanders; a promenade gives onto a small bay with natural swimming pools.

São Sebastião ★

This modest village is the site of the first settlement on the island. The Gothic church dates from 1455 and has a fine doorway and interior vaulting in Renaissance and Manueline styles. Nearby, the **Império do Espírito Santo** sits on a street corner decorated in bright colours.

Serra do Cume ★

Not always worth visiting because of low clouds, the Serra do Cume is the remains of an eroded volcano, its slopes forming a symmetrical pattern of walled fields. On a clear

Praia da Vitória

Not to Scale

day, the view is quite extensive, and worth the drive up; in fact, with an altitude of 545m (1788ft), Serra do Cume has one of the most extensive panoramic views on the island. To the east lies the bay of Praia da Vitória and the Lajes plain, while to the west is the extensive interior of the island characterized by the hundreds of size-variable *cerrados* or enclosed fields partitioned by black stone walls or hedgerows of blue hydrangea.

PRAIA DA VITÓRIA **

Much smaller than Angra do Heroísmo, Praia – its name derives from a superb white sand beach that reaches all around the bay – is today the main port for heavy shipping, but this is set at some distance from the town, and does not detract from the lively and popular attraction of the place. The town is well designed, with a large central square. Much of the old town has been preserved, and is a pleasure to wander around. The parish church was founded by the island's first donee-captain, Jacomo de Bruges. The doorway was a gift from King Dom Manuel, and the interior is renowned for its *azulejos* and gilt altar work.

LAJES *

The elongated village of Lajes is one of the oldest on the island, and has a black-and-white *império* and an attractive church.

GASTRONOMY

There are a number of traditional dishes on Terceira, including the Holy Spirit soup (*sopa do Espírito Santo*), fish stew with apple (*caldeirada de peixe com maçãs*), black pudding (*morcela*) and stewed rabbit (*coelho em molho vilão*). Crab, barnacles and limpets are prepared according to traditional recipes. Whether you like the limpets or barnacles is something you have to chew over. Most meals begin even before you order your food, when a small, freshly made goat's cheese is brought to your table; you pay for it, of course, but it is only a nominal charge.

If you have a sweet tooth, try the sugar biscuits, *alfenim* or *donas amélias*, or the fritters (*coscorões*) and *massa sovada*, a sweet bread.

Opposite: *Calcareous roof formation, Algar do Carvão.*

FOLKLORE

The folklore of Terceira is varied and features traditional Azorean dances and melancholic songs. Many villages have their own folk groups who intentionally or otherwise maintain these important cultural traditions. Rising above the melancholy are the more cheerful *cantares ao desafio*, a form of popular ballad in which the singers improvize the lyrics, often ironic or satirical.

Biscoitos *

The small village of Biscoitos is renowned for its vineyards, or *curraletas*, protected by basaltic walls beneath which they flourish. The **Museu do Vinho**, founded in 1990, has displays of wine-making equipment – cellars, stills, presses and baskets – that produce the wine *verdelho*. The wine museum is also the seat of the Confraria do Vinho Verdelho, an institution set up with the aim of preserving the integrity and quality of *verdelho* and other Azorean wines; in that respect it is admirably successful. Open April–September daily 09:00–19:00; October–March 10:00–16:00 (closed Sunday and Monday).

The name *biscoitos* has been given to lava formations that produce an almost lunar landscape along the coast. Nearby **natural swimming pools** are popular during the summer months. The coastline is lined with **fortifications** used to defend the islands against pirate attacks in the 16th and 17th centuries.

Furnas do Enxofre *

Although holding no comparison with the fumaroles on São Miguel, the Furnas do Enxofre in the centre of the island south of the Pico Alto volcano is nevertheless a Regional Natural Monument. This is an area that emits noxious volcanic gases – mainly carbon dioxide, sulphidic and sulphurous gases, hydrogen, nitrogen and methane – at temperatures up to 95°C (203°F) at the surface. As a result of this steady gas emission, the surrounding rocks are constantly in a state of change, as is the adjacent vegetation which not only has to cope with the gases, but also altitude (up to 620m/2034ft), humidity and an annual rainfall of 2m (79 in). Not surprisingly, the area has a tendency to become swamp-like. On the hillside to the northeast of the fumaroles some interesting vegetation exists, notably the Azorean holly, Azorean laurel and juniper, all endemic species, while many of the species of fern and dogwood are listed in the Red Data Book of endangered species.

Visually, the Furnas do Enxofre does not have a 'Wow' factor, but its importance to the ecology of the island cannot be questioned.

ALGAR DO CARVÃO ★★★

Located not far from the Furnas do Enxofre, at 550m (1804ft) above sea level, the cave at Algar do Carvão, virtually at the centre of the island, deserves to be better known; this is a Regional Natural Monument, and rightly so. In the context of large holes in the ground it is, essentially, a large hole in the ground. In fact, it is a volcanic chimney, formed by escaping gases when the lava cooled. But it is a quite spectacular hole in the ground, approached through a long descending tunnel before you emerge, already some way down the hole, just below the fern and moss line, and on the edge of the huge cavern with walls and ceiling draped in stalactites formed by siliceous accretions that quite take you by surprise.

Parts of the cave date from around 2000BP, while the oldest and largest section is associated with the Pico Alto volcano, active around 3200BP. Botanists rave about the quality of the cave, and the flora covering the cone which includes 34 different liverwort species, 22 species of moss and 27 vascular plants. To the less specialized tourist, this means lush vegetation that is, nevertheless, impressive.

Steps lead down through various levels of overlapping arches to just above the lake that lies at the bottom of the cave. Multi-hued walls – beige, black, grey, green – soar above and below, and soft musak gives the visit a mildly eerie quality. This is never going to be a cavern to rival the best in the world, but it would be a pity to miss it. As the vegetation holds a lot of moisture, it follows that there is a constant but gentle rainfall in the cave, so take a waterproof jacket. There is a small admission charge; opening hours are variable, but arrive midday and there should be no problem.

Terceira at a Glance

July and **August** are the most popular months, but **spring** is a good time just as the flowers come into bloom, and the months from April to October when there is a freshness in the air. In **summer**, the temperature can rise to 27°C (81°F), but seldom higher. There is **rainfall** in every month, but for the most part it is not long lasting. **Humidity** is within a narrow range, 80–85%, but can increase to 100%.

SATA Air Açores fly to Terceira from all the other islands; in fact, Terceira is usually the intermediary island between many of the others, with flights calling in here en route to somewhere else. **TAP** flies direct to Terceira from Lisbon, and via Lisbon from London Gatwick and Heathrow.

It is easy to get round the island by car in a day, and a useful way of doing this, as with the other islands, is to use a taxi. The drivers are knowledgeable, and can point out things that may otherwise be missed. They also know the good places to eat.

There is an excellent range of hotels on Terceira, although most of these tend to be concentrated in Angra do Heroísmo and Praia da Vitória.

Angra do Heroísmo

Hotel Caracol, Estrada Regional, Silveira, 9700-193, tel: 295 402 600, www.hotel docaracol.com Excellent hotel to the west of the city, about 20 minutes' brisk walk from the centre. Fine views. Good standard restaurant, bar, Wellness Centre with spa, thalassotherapy and physiotherapy, sauna, Turkish bath, two gymnasia, indoor swimming pool, squash court, outdoor swimming pool and kids' pool. Direct access to the sea.
Terra Mar Hotel, overlooking Silveira Bay, tel: 296 301 880. Smart, sizeable, 20 minutes from the centre.
Angra Garden Hotel, Praça Velha, 9700-201, tel: 295 206 600, www.angrahotel.com Right in the heart of the historical centre, and backing on to the Angra Gardens; 120 rooms, including six suites, restaurant, bar, lounge, and a Health Club with gym, sauna, Turkish bath, Jacuzzi and indoor pool.
Residencial Globo, Rua do Galo, 26/28, 9700-091, tel: 295 213 691. Right in the centre of the city; rooms with private bathrooms and cable TV.
Praia da Vitória
Hotel Praia Marina, Ave. Beira Mar, 9760-412, tel: 295 540 055, fax: 295 540 056, www.hotelpraiamarina.com Just 50m from the main square and even closer to the beach. Offers a range of rooms, suites and apartments in a very modern context. Bar and free park-

ing, but no restaurant as there are quite a few within a few minutes' walking distance.
Varandas do Atlântico, Rua da Alfândega 19, 9760-411, tel: 295 540 050, www.hotel varandas.com No frills, but with 30 rooms, some with balconies and the possibility of connecting rooms.
Hotel Residencial Terezinha, Praceta Dr Machado Pires 45, 9760-449, tel: 295 540 060, fax: 295 542 202, www.hotel teresinha.net Just 3km (2 miles) from the airport, and 500m from the beach. Fifty rooms, garden, outdoor pool. Peaceful and quiet.
São Sebastião, Canada do Funcho, 9700-644 Salga, São Sebastião, tel: 295 905 034, fax: 295 905 035, www.rural salga.com Country home with seven rooms, ocean view, veranda and swimming pool. A few minutes from Salga's natural swimming pools.
Youth Hostels
Pousada de Juventude de Angra do Heroísmo, Negrito, São Mateus, 9760-554 Angra do Heroísmo, tel/fax: 295 642 095, www.pousadasjuven tude.pt Seventy beds in multiple rooms plus one apartment with WC, kitchen and lounge.
Camping
There are a number of camping sites around Terceira at Salga, near Porto Judeu, Porto de San Fernando, Biscoitos and Ponta das Cinco. Standards vary, but in a basic way are quite acceptable.

Terceira at a Glance

There is a whole raft of places to eat in Angra do Heroísmo, although there are fewer places, other than small bar-restaurants, the more you wander round the island.

Angra do Heroísmo
Restaurant Cozinha do Caracol. Within the Hotel Caracol (*see* Where to Stay), and often with a buffet. Lunchtime Table d'Hote menu and evening à la carte serving fish and meat dishes in some imaginative combinations. Relaxing, friendly ambience.
Marcelino's Bar Steak House, Rua de São João, 9700-182, tel: 295 215 828. If it's steak you want, this is the place.
Restaurant Bom Garío, Rua de São João, 9700-182, tel: 295 333 286. Not far from the Steak House, serves grilled fish.
Praia da Vitória
Marcelino's Bar Steak House, Rua 1 Conde Siúve de Meneses 6, 9760-439.
O Pescador Restaurant, Rua Constantino José Cardoso 11, 9760-441, tel: 295 513 495. Fish, what else with a name like that? Well, meat, too.
Porto Martins
Restaurant Búzius, tel: 295 515 5555. Described as a 'Casa da Picanha', which is a Brazilian meat dish, but also promotes its Italian cuisine.
Altares
Restaurante Caneta, Às Presas, Estrada Regional Altares 9700 Angra do Heroísmo, tel: 295 989 162.

Don't be fooled by the Angra do Heroísmo address; Altares is on the north coast and ideally placed for a lunch halt if you are touring the island. Bar-snack bar at street level, but excellent upstairs restaurant serving fish and meat dishes, and good wine (none served by the glass). Specialities include grilled octopus and home-made black pudding – the house beef steak (*Bifa da Casa*) is a good choice. Parking is round the corner, in a side street.

Twin's Disco, Rua Diogo de Teive, 54, 9700-065 Angra do Heroísmo, tel: 962 925 361 or 962 926 471, www.twins clubdisco.com Opens midnight, closes 06:00, summertime, Thu, Fri and Sat.

The centre of Angra do Heroísmo is an excellent place to shop; the streets from the marina up into the old town centre are lined with many shops selling both traditional Azorean items and quality produce. Check to ensure that items are not imported from the east, or otherwise cost more than necessary.
Azulart, Estr. Dr Marcelino Moules 78, 9700-321 Cinco Ribeiras, tel: 295 907 034. This is the place to go for regional ceramic tiles from

Terceira island, turned on the potter's wheel and hand-painted.

Flight Sightseeing
Aero Clube da Ilha Terceira, Aerogare Civil das Lajes, 9760-251 Praia da Vitória, tel: 295 512 031/4.
Whale Watching and Adventure Tours
Carlos Lima, Marina Praia da Vitória, tel: 295 542 482, mobile: 966 370 498.
Graturmar, Avenida Conde Sieuve de Meneses 37-A, 9700-056 Angra do Heroísmo, tel: 962 734 542, www.graturmar.com.sapo.pt
Marsol, tel: 961 117 210 or 295 663 915.
Adventure Sports
Octopus Diving Centre, Clube Náutico de Angra do Heroísmo, Estrada Gaspar Corte Real, 9700-030 Angra do Heroísmo, tel: 964 575 565, www.octopusportugal.com Scuba diving.

Tourist Office
Terceira: Rua Direita 70/74, 9700-066 Angra do Heroísmo, tel: 295 213 393, fax: 295 212 922, email: turter@mail.telepac.pt
Biscoitos: Museu do Vinho, Casa Agrícola Brum Biscoitos, Canada do Caldeiro, 9760, Praia da Vitória.
Terceira Island Environment Department, tel: 295 206 310.

5
Graciosa

The name Graciosa is said to derive from 'gracious', an appellation accorded to Santa Cruz. There is certainly a gracious aspect about the island, which, but for Corvo, would be the smallest of the archipelago. It is vital that visitors to the Azores head for the principal islands, but if only one of the smaller islands of the central group can be included, this should be it. Graciosa is so unlike any of the other islands, not just the main ones. There is an agreeable quality of restfulness, gentility and otherworldliness that rests over the island like a mantle of serenity. The pace of life is slow and easy, and the island has retained its rural charm and an atmosphere of calm isolation. Along the village streets farmers still use horse and cart to get about, or donkeys (jokingly called the Azorean Jaguar) – although that menace of intensive farming in other countries, the quad bike, is beginning to appear on the streets of the islands, needlessly many locals consider. Men still gather on street corners to chat companionably, or in the bars to play dominoes.

Graciosa is the least humid of the Azorean islands, and manages to reach an altitude of only 398m (1305ft) in Pico Timão, prompting a tendency for all the villages to be rather evenly spaced both around the coast and across the interior. The landscape in the lower areas is subdivided into hundreds of stonewall plots to protect the vines and other produce from the winds that can visit the islands in winter. The villages, for the most part, are bright and colourful, with groups of whitewashed houses clustered around the village church, and red-topped Dutch-style **windmills** dotted around a patterned countryside of pastures and allotments: wholly delightful.

DON'T MISS

*** **Caldeira:** the highest point of the island drapes itself around a massive *caldeira*.
*** **Furna do Enxofre:** huge sulphur cavern.
** **Carapacho:** perfect for sea bathing in its natural swimming pool.
** **Praia:** essentially a pleasant fishing port with a small marina.
** **Farol da Ponta da Barca:** visit this lighthouse and discover a great view of the whale rock, Baleia.

Opposite: *The coastline of Graciosa provides splendid images of crashing waves and multi-hued volcanic rocks: Porta da Barca.*

VITAL STATISTICS

Graciosa has an area of 62km² (24 sq miles) and a population of 4838 (2006). The island is 12.5km (8 miles) by 8.5km (5 miles), and is roughly oval in shape. The main centre is Santa Cruz.

Given the proximity of the neighbouring island of Terceira, it is probable that Graciosa was first discovered from there, but there is no evidence to substantiate this. It is difficult to be certain about the early discoveries of these central islands, and in any case, so much depends on what is meant by 'discovered'; sometimes things get lost in translation for it is certain that if you 'discover' any one of the central group then given decent weather conditions you 'discover' all the rest. Certainly from Graciosa you can see Terceira, São Jorge above which rises the summit of Pico, and off to the west, Faial. Most likely, but unproveable, is the suggestion that the existence of the central islands, as with the eastern islands and for that matter Madeira and Porto Santo, was known by sailors in the 14th century, but only 'officially' discovered and settled when to do so brought honour and distinction to the enterprising Prince Henry the Navigator, who is the central figure throughout the discovery of these Atlantic islands. What lends credence to this notion is an extract in *Saudades da Terra* by historian Gaspar Frutuoso which relates how 'Pedro Correia, Nobleman in the books of the King and of Correias of the realm, was given news of the appearance of

Graciosa Island. He asked for the king's permission to discover it...he arrived on Terceira Island in the boat in which he would go in search of Graciosa, and he departed to discover the island, and, having found it, he ordered a Mass to be said there, and all called it Graciosa Island.' So, basically, you know somewhere exists, but need the monarch's permission to discover it. Until you get permission, it remains undiscovered, which is a neat piece of historical jiggery-pokery.

Left: *A small chapel overlooking Santa Cruz da Graciosa proves an ideal vantage point from which to study the layout of the town.*

What *is* known is that Graciosa's first settler was Vasco Gil Sodré who came from Montemor-o-Velho in Portugal along with his family and servants to settle at Carpacho. Certainly he was the one responsible for first clearing large tracts of vegetation. There is uncertainty about the date of Sodré's arrival, but historians now believe this was 1475. Moreover, later research establishes the date on which Santa Cruz was elevated to a township as 1486 and not 1500 as some accounts relate.

The fertility of the island's soil was of key importance in establishing Graciosa as a producer of **cereals** and **vines**. Within a century of the first settlement, the people of the island were already sending barley, wheat and wine to neighbouring islands. Such productivity, however, attracted the attention of pirates, and grain would often have to be stored in underground chambers. Today, fishing and cattle farming, along with the production of grapes, are the mainstays of the island's economy. Tourism is on the increase, but as elsewhere throughout the Azores much needs to be done to energize the essential infrastructure.

A TASTE OF GRACIOSA

Fish soup: The fish used to make this soup is grouper, which has a white and tasty flesh; the dish, almost stewed, also today uses some pasta which replaces the potato that is used in the traditional recipe.

In 2007 a large, cleared patch of earth marked the location of the island's first hotel, a four-star **Hotel da Graciosa** near the coast in Santa Cruz, involving an investment of €6 million. While building strategies suggested completion in 10 months, local realists suggest that 2009 would be nearer the mark. Either way, the hotel will be a vital addition to the island's resources for tourists, but the fact that it has taken so long to build a hotel here is an indication of how slowly tourism has developed, or how reluctant the venture capitalists have been with their money.

Santa Cruz ★★

Santa Cruz is certainly the largest of the towns on the island, a delightful place set around ancient watering holes for cattle that are today flanked by young **dragon trees**. The adjacent cobbled square, scene of numerous festivities, is usually a peaceful place to relax after dinner – give or take the odd quad bike roaring by. Beyond and around the ponds lie a number of elegant mansions and the church, **Igreja Matriz de Santa Cruz da Graciosa**, built towards the end of the 15th century in the Gothic style, characteristic of the reign of King Dom Manuel I. Academics consider that this church, which contains **16th-century paintings** of some significance, is among the finest churches in all of the Azorean islands.

Right: *Graciosa Museum, containing a collection of items of local interest.*

Left: *The main church of Santa Cruz, the Igreja Matriz de Santa Cruz da Graciosa, is typical of the architectural style of most churches across the islands.*

Down by the old harbour you find **fishermen's cottages** redolent of the times of whaling. There are a number of bars around the square, and shops and cafés in the side streets. It is worth wandering along some of the streets to admire the architecture of the town's houses, many of which have the wrought-iron balconies that are so graciously typical of the Azores.

Graciosa Museum ★★

Focusing largely on Graciosa, of course, the museum contains a collection of items of local interest, mainly musical instruments and implements used in wine production. Established in 1983, the museum is housed in a traditional building from the 19th century that would have been used by wealthy local traders for storing corn, or making wine.

Just across the road from the museum is the **old harbour**, a tiny place where you can walk down to the water's edge and consider life in the days when whaling boats would have launched from here.

On a bluff overlooking the town, of which there is a splendid view, stands the 16th-century **Chapel of Nossa Senhora da Ajuda**. It also provides a good vantage point for the bullring below, but it is likely that the local people have already thought of that!

FESTIVALS IN GRACIOSA

As with all the islands in the group, there are small festivals in each of the villages throughout the summer – any excuse to party. Across the island, but less so than in Terceira, are the elegant *impérios*, chapels to the Holy Spirit. Of particular interest on the festival front is the **Festival of Espírito Santo** on the seventh Sunday after Easter; this takes place widely over the island, but a little more enthusiastically in Santa Cruz, Guadalupe, Luz and São Mateus. The **Festival of Santo Cristo** held in early August involves boat races, bullfights (the bullring is on the hill overlooking Santa Cruz), music and dancing. This is a particularly exciting time, luring emigrants back from America and Canada to join in the celebrations.

Graciosa is famous for its fish, and you may like to try the **seafood stew** with rice (*Arroz de Mariscos*); it's messy but delicious. Fish comes in a variety of ways – grilled, stewed or baked. Local beef is good, too, as are **spicy pork sausages** such as *linquiça* (usually served as a starter) and blood sausage, or kale soup with meat.

Seafood is plentiful with lobster, crab, mussels and prawns all available from around the island.

Graciosa is also famous for its **wines**, producing light, fruity red and white wines that have a low alcohol rating. If you like a sweet drink to finish your meal, try *angelica* or a passion fruit liqueur (*maracuja*); otherwise sample the local brandy, *aguardente*. In fact, a tiny splash of brandy in a meal-end coffee makes the otherwise very strong coffee much more palatable.

If you follow the coastline anticlockwise from Santa Cruz you soon reach the **lighthouse**, **Farol da Ponta da Barca**. From here you get a good view of **Baleia**, the so-called whale rock just offshore, that does resemble a large whale, with a little imagination. Attractive villages grace the landscape like jewels in an ornate necklace, with **Guadalupe**, a pleasing village with traditional white cottages set amid a patchwork of cultivated fields, very much at the centre of the island.

CALDEIRA ★★★

The highest point of the island drapes itself around a massive *caldeira*, the cone of an extinct volcano forming an inner elliptical crater with an asymmetric rim defined by steep walls; you only realize how steep-sided and extensive this crater is once actually in it. The whole of the crater is covered in lush vegetation in which sound carries remarkably; it is a restful spot, disturbed only by the sound of visitors heading down to the crater's heart at Furna do Enxofre (*see* below).

FURNA DO ENXOFRE ★★★

For a nominal payment visitors can, as on Terceira, descend into the bowels of the earth. This huge cavern lies at the heart of a massive volcanic crater. A tunnel has been dug through the crater walls to allow access by car to the entrance to the chasm. From here you set off down a gently sloping pathway to the top of a constructed spiral staircase (and, it must be said, something of a ghastly intrusion – the same problem has been resolved far more sensitively on Terceira). The 183 steps, constructed in 1939, now lead down to the cave, 220m (722ft) by 120m (394ft). At the very bottom, beyond a roped-off area, is a cold sulphurous lake, and nearby a small opening in which hot mud bubbles and gurgles; in the silence of the huge cave, this is quite an eerie sound. The cave is impressive, with multi-hued walls decked in lichen and siliceous deposits.

Discovered as long ago as the 15th century, in 1879 the cave was visited by Prince Albert of Monaco, a noted oceanographer, who had to descend into the cave on a rope ladder. Take time to consider how that must have felt; and then set off back up those 183 steps. Prince Albert was so impressed, he returned on a number of occasions.

Sometimes the amount of sulphur gas given off is too high to permit people to enter the cave. This is most likely to happen in winter, but there is no way of anticipating this, or of knowing whether you will gain admission, until you get there. If you are unfortunate enough to be turned away, then time spent exploring this vast crater will not be wasted. Both the cave and the crater make a memorable experience, something in awe of which it does no harm to be.

CARAPACHO **

Mentioned below for its good natural swimming pool, excellent coastal scenery with islands, and a fine place to eat, Carapacho is also the location of **thermal baths** where visitors can just bob around for a relaxing 15-minute dip – egg timers beside the baths let you know when you're done. The spa, which makes use of hot springs that rise from the sea bed for therapeutic purposes, was renovated

Left: *The clear waters off the coast at Carapacho are perfect for sea bathing; a nearby thermal spa only adds to the attraction of this corner of the island.*

Right: *This brightly deco-rated* réligio – *most numerous on Terceira – stands at the centre of the fishing port of Praia.*

in 1993, and has 20 individual bathrooms. In 2007, the spa was promised funding to ensure an extension and upgrade to the present facility, which will make this tiny village even more appealing. There is a good retrospective view of the village from near the **lighthouse** on the hill above. The coastline here is especially attractive: steep cliffs fall to the sea, and small islands complete a picture many photographers will want to capture.

PRAIA ★★
Praia is essentially a fishing port with a small marina, and the customary cobbled square at its centre. The beach here is lovely white sand and hugely popular.

Those in search of somewhere ideal to go **swimming** might consider the open-air swimming pool at Santa Cruz, the beach at Praia, or the easily accessed natural swimming area at Carapacho; in fact, Carapacho is becoming very popular, not least because it also has superb coastal scenery, a good restaurant (*see* the 'Dolphin', in 'Where to Eat', page 77) and modern apartments to rent for short-duration stays at economical prices. Surfing, in spite of some ideal-looking waves, can be dangerous where the waves break against lavic rocks. Windsurfing, however, is popular at a number of locations, especially Santa Cruz and Praia. Diving, not surprisingly, yields wonderful under-water sights in the clear water, while fishing by line, from boat or shore, rarely fails to produce something to eat.

Graciosa at a Glance

SATA Air Açores fly to Graciosa from Terceira, which acts as a hub.
It is possible to get a **ferry** from Terceira to Graciosa and from Graciosa to the next nearest island, São Jorge, direct. Times are variable according to the season, but the latest information is available through the website www.transmacor.pt

The bus services are geared to providing for local people. A timetable is available at the tourist office in Santa Cruz, or get one at your guesthouse. It is worth considering taking the bus to your planned destination, and then calling a taxi to bring you back. The roads are generally very good, and local traffic is fairly light, so think about picking up a rental car at the airport on arrival (pre-book it first). Otherwise, the best way to get around is to use taxis, which are inexpensive, or to book a taxi for a tour of the island.

There are, as yet, no hotels on Graciosa. Until the new hotel under construction in 2007 is complete, you will have to find a guesthouse (*pensão*) in which to stay (Graciosa is far too agreeable to miss).
Pensão (Residencial) Ilha Graciosa, Ave Mouzinho de Albuquerque 49, 9880-320

Santa Cruz da Graciosa, tel: 295 712 675. Restored manor house, 10 minutes' walk from the town square. Spacious grounds and two tennis courts. Comfortable lounge and bar/breakfast room, 16 rooms, TV and direct dial telephone. Wireless Internet (charged).
Pensão (Residencial) Santa Cruz, Largo Barão de Guadalupe, 9880-344 Santa Cruz da Graciosa, tel: 295 712 345. Eighteen rooms with satellite TV and direct dial telephone. Close to the town centre, and the sea.

You can rent a **windmill** on a weekly basis at **Boina de Vento**, Casa de Campo, Rua dos Moinhos de Vento 44, 9880-280 São Mateus, tel: 295 732 133, www.boinade vento.com It is also possible to rent modern apartments owned by the government at Carapacho – contact the tourist information office in Santa Cruz for information.
Camping
There are camp sites at Cais da Barra (Santa Cruz – basic but free), Barro Vermelho and Alta do Sul.

Santa Cruz
Apolo 80, Rua Dr João VI 12, 9880-375 Santa Cruz da Graciosa. On the edge of the main square, serving fish and meat dishes. A good place to try the seafood and rice dish (*Arroz de Mariscos*), or a variety of local fish dishes. Tends

to be a bit noisy on Saturdays. Excellent range of Portuguese wines. No English menu.
Rivoli, Ave Mouzinho de Albuquerque 38, 9880-320 Santa Cruz da Graciosa, tel: 295 732 456. Simple, clean and bright café serving snacks, light lunches (not on Sundays) and sandwiches.
Praia
Restaurant Marisqueira, Rua Fontes Pereira de Melo 148, 9880-235 São Mateus, Praia, tel: 295 732 855. Very popular eatery serving a good selection of traditional cuisine. You may have to wait for a table at weekends, or make a reservation, but it is well worth it. The wine list has many excellent Portuguese wines and a selection from the Azores.
Carapacho
Dolphin, Carapacho 16, 9880-120 Luz, tel: 295 712 014. Bright restaurant with terrace overlooking the sea. Very popular. Ask your hotel to make a reservation. Good range of seafood dishes; a good place to try Graciosa wines.

Scuba Diving and Snorkelling
Centre Nautico Graciosa, tel/fax: 295 732 811, www.divinggraciosa.com

Tourist Office
Rua da Boavista 9, 9980-377 Santa Cruz da Graciosa, tel: 295 712 509, fax: 295 732 446.

6
São Jorge

The island of São Jorge is almost entirely a plateau with 700m (2297ft) high cliffs; the exceptions are the *fajãs*, which are platforms nearer sea level, resulting from land slides, and which, paradoxically, if a little crazily, provided space for housing and farming. Because of their location most have a micro-climate that favours the production of tropical fruits – the dragon trees seem to like it, too.

Basically, the island is a long sausage with steep sides and pointed ends. Just about everywhere there are stunning seascapes and coastal scenery where verdant cliffs of many greens plunge almost vertically to the sea. Here and there small villages of whitewashed houses and colourful buildings cling to the edges, sandwiched between cliff and sea. In places, attractive houses betray a certain level of prosperity, but elsewhere horses and donkeys are the principal mode of transport for many of the local people.

It is not known when São Jorge was first settled, but it is thought to have been around 1443. Certainly, by 1460 there was already a nucleus of people living in the area of what is now the town of Velas, which today is the main centre. Around 1480, another centre of population grew up at the eastern end of the island, at Topo, largely under the influence of a Flemish nobleman, Willem van der Haghen (which he later changed to Guilherme da Silveira). In 1483, João Vaz Corte Real was appointed donee-captain.

By the second half of the 16th century, São Jorge had a population of 3000, settled in or around three towns: Velas, Topo and Calheta. During the early stages of the island's development, wheat was the main crop produced,

DON'T MISS

*** Velas: a delightful main town of cobbled streets and wrought-iron balconies.
*** Ponta do Topo: the eastern end of the island; remote and quite splendid.
** The *fajãs*: remarkable isolated villages of rural charm.
** São Jorge cheese: highly regarded and with great taste.
** Sete Fontes Forest Park: the Forest Park of the Seven Fountains is a delightful place for a picnic.
** Rosais and Ponta dos Rosais: splendid walking at the western end of the island, and a lovely linear village.

Opposite: *Fashionable and typical, wrought-iron balcony, Velas.*

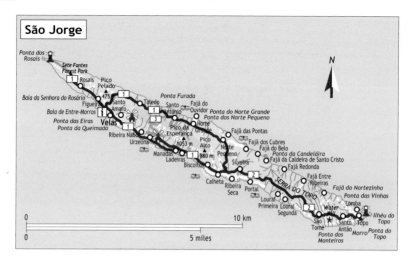

followed by vines. From there the island and its people went on to develop a small but prosperous society based on the growth and exportation to Flanders of woad for use in the dye industry.

The peaceful way of life of the islanders was shattered by volcanic eruptions (these took place in 1580, 1757 and 1808), and, later, by numerous pirate attacks, one in particular, in 1625, when Algerian pirates attacked São João, taking the inhabitants for slaves. The island suffered during a volcanic eruption in 1808, when lava destroyed all but one church tower at **Urzelina**. On the northern side of the island, **Fajã do Ouvidor** is clearly the product of lava flows rather than land slip responsible for most of the other *fajãs*.

During the early part of the 19th century, São Jorge enjoyed the wealth that came from orange growing and wine production, as well as whaling, and you can still see the occasional whale lookouts on various headlands. The island, like Terceira and Graciosa, was badly affected by the earthquake in 1980, and around the island gaunt overgrown ruins remain a testimony to this brief but life-shattering experience.

With so much excellent grazing land, it is not surprising that today the economy of the island is based on cattle

---

A TASTE OF SÃO JORGE

Fried cheese with raspberry jam: Simply fried and served warm with raspberry jam as an accompaniment; this dish has always been served on São Jorge, although it is not exclusive to the island.

rearing and dairy produce, especially the cheeses for which the island is justly renowned.

São Jorge is delightfully green, as a day tour will reveal, lush vegetation mantles the sea slopes and wild flowers, hibiscus, hydrangea, morning glory, evening primrose, ginger lily and belladonna lily grow in profusion.

VELAS **

If there is a main town then Velas is it, a neat enclave backed by a steep cliff. The town layout isn't exactly grid pattern, but, being small, it is not difficult to understand and follow. There is a large **supermarket** here and a number of small shops selling everyday items and souvenirs. The buildings are particularly attractive, and many of them have the emblematic Azorean **wrought-iron balconies** which are here in better condition than on other islands. Some of the central area has been pedestrianized and the street paved with the black-and-white blocks of basalt and limestone fashioned into local scenes. The **town hall** is an imposing example of 16th-century Azorean architecture; it stands opposite an attractive garden (complete with bandstand) that serves as a meeting place for local men. The area around the harbour is attractive in a typical harbour messy kind of way, and here you find the 18th-century gateway, the **Portão do Mar**, the gate of the sea.

VITAL STATISTICS

The island lies 40km (25 miles) south of Graciosa and 20km (12.5 miles) north of Pico; it is 56km (35 miles) long, but only 8km (5 miles) wide, with a total area of 246 km² (95 sq miles) and a population of 9504 (2006). The highest point of the island is Pico de Esperança at 1053m (3455ft). The climate is mild with little humidity.

Left: *The main street in Velas is a bright arrangement of street cafés and Azorean architecture.*

FAJÃS

The word *fajã* means a small, flat piece of agricultural land near the sea. There are 46 *fajãs* on the island, many quite small. Thirty lie on the north coast and the rest on the south, and for the most part at the base of high escarpments. Traditionally they were cultivated, with enormous effort, over the centuries, but many were abandoned after the 1980 earthquake, and today only the larger ones are inhabited. *Fajãs* were formed either as a result of lava flows or land-slides, and those that are abandoned offer the visitor a chance to discover the houses, mills and fountains used by the people that lived in these remote places. Transhumance, the pasturing of cattle here, was also prac-tised for many years.

Not so far from this culturally endearing other-worldliness, the area around the library, the hotel, the theatre and the **church of São Jorge** announces its place in the 21st century. It is this delightful interplay of old and new, and the town's setting on a large *fajã* set against imposing cliffs, that make Velas such an attractive resort.

On the way east, towards Urzelina, there is a fine view-point with an excellent aerial aspect of Velas. The name **Urzelina** recalls a time when the economy of the island rested on gathering lichen (*urzela*) for use in the dyeing process. There is, too, another link with the past: in a small garden the remains of a church bell tower is all that remains of the 1808 volcanic eruption that swept away the rest of the church and much of the village, which had to be rebuilt. That same eruption created a small group of caves at the water's edge that can be visited on boat tours from the port.

Further east you reach **Manadas** and the **Church of Santa Bárbara** which is especially important not so much for its external appearance but for the intricate gold deco-ration of its interior. This lavish display of religious art and finely worked cedarwood ceiling is regarded as one of the

Right: *A street plaque in Urzelina.*

most important in the Azores. The road is a delight to follow, clinging as it does to the base of cliffs with a lovely view across to the simple, almost childlike cone shape of Pico Alto. Along the way, if you divert sufficiently, you encounter a number of the **windmills** that are typical of São Jorge; a simplistic design, with many windmills having just a single blade rather than two. A viewpoint at **Ladeiras** offers good views of the island's south coast, before reaching **Biscoitos**, another neat village tacked onto what little ground there is between cliff and sea.

Calheta *

A rather more substantial place with rows of houses seemingly overhanging the sea, Calheta, second in size only to Velas and constructed on Fajã Grande, is a good place to pause. A stroll through this town will reveal groups of 18th- and 19th-century buildings, notably in the Largo do Cais. The **Museum of São Jorge** is in a house built in 1811, and contains both a permanent collection – a bedroom, living room and kitchen, and agricultural implements – and a wide-ranging bibliographical collection on the history and traditions of the island.

From Calheta the road runs across the top of the island, crossing the Serra do Topo before descending to **Santo Antão**, and running on to the end of the island at Ponto do Topo. Just before completing the descent to **Topo** there is a stunning view down to its lighthouse and the flat **Ilhéu do Topo** a short distance offshore and used for pasturing cattle; sheep were taken across in boats, but the cattle had to swim, tethered to the boat. All around Topo there are numerous black stone walls and corrals in which vines are grown. This end of the island is one of the first places to be settled, and today it is an agreeable little town with fine mansions, a church, an *império* and a small fishing port approached by an impossibly steep road.

Ilhéu do Topo **

There are no organized means of getting to this island, although local fishermen may well agree to take you over. But the island is a Natura 2000 Special Protection Area

Natura 2000 on São Jorge

The Natura 2000 network (see page 10 in the Introduction) on São Jorge embraces the Ilhéu do Topo, which is a Special Protection Area, and two Sites of Community Importance: Ponta dos Rosais, and the North Coast and Ponta do Topo.

Right: *The extreme eastern end of São Jorge – Ponta do Topo – is both inviting and relaxing; off-shore the Ilhéu do Topo is a specially protected area.*

due to the importance of the bird fauna found here, notably the roseate tern, common tern, Cory's shearwater and the Azores woodpigeon. Check with the São Jorge Environmental Department first (tel: 292 628 220) to see if you need permission to cross. The SPA also includes a length of main island coastline between Morro, south of Topo, to Fajã do Nortezinho.

This end of the island is quite magical, and the viewing area overlooking Ilhéu do Topo is somewhere you can while away many peaceable hours watching birds and listening to the waves and the eerie call of the shearwater, a sound that defies description (unless you have heard an Australian Iggly-Wiggly Ball – in which case you know *exactly* what a Cory's shearwater sounds like).

THE NORTHEAST COAST AND PONTA DO TOPO ★★★

Designated a Site of Community Importance, the northeast coast of São Jorge is breathtaking. Near-vertical cliffs rise 700m (2296ft) from the sea and are a spectacular sight as you fly in from Terceira. At the base of the cliffs are the many *fajãs*, mainly the result of land slip, and here you find small populations eking a tenuous living from the sea and land. What makes the coast so special in ecological terms is the diversity from areas of active raised bog and natural forest to biologically rich, shallow marine areas with reefs and open bays. Here you find the only system of coastal lagoon in the Azores, wholly or partially separated from the

---

THE WINDMILLS

The design of the windmills on São Jorge is quite unique, set on tall, narrow bases in the form of a truncated cone, and painted in bright colours or simply white. Unlike more conventional windmills, instead of sails, the windmills of São Jorge have blades, either one or two. These relatively modern windmills have replaced the timber windmills positioned on a wheel that ground wheat here for centuries. And, in spite of such progress, even these are now becoming obsolete, redundant artefacts for tourists.

sea by sand banks and shingle. Juniper grows abundantly here, along with the endemic pink bell-like flower *Azorina vidallii* along with an Azorean subspecies of heather. The sea around the coast is favoured by loggerhead turtle, harbour porpoise and bottlenose dolphin.

NORTE PEQUENO **

The village of Norte Pequeno is an uncomplicated settlement typical of the islands, but greater interest lies along the coast to the east, where a walking route links the Fajã da Caldeira do Santo Cristo, the smaller Fajã do Belo and the Fajã dos Cubres. You don't have to do the walk to appreciate the setting: there is a fine viewpoint overlooking the **Fajã dos Cubres**. From here the road continues down to the sea between sheer drops covered in lush vegetation. At the bottom, a semicircle of flat ground surrounds a small lake and all around is the sea, breaking in foam on the shingle beach. Further along lies the **Fajã da Caldeira de Santo Cristo**, which has a slightly larger lake, the only place in the Azores producing what are called cockles, but are in fact clams (*ameijoes*).

NORTE GRANDE **

As the name suggests, Norte Grande is a little larger than Norte Pequeno, but remains otherwise very similar. Again, the interest lies along the coast at **Fajã do Ouvidor**, where there is a more substantial settlement of white houses scattered across the fields planted with potatoes, sweet corn, beans and vines that produce grapes from which they make *vinho de cheiro*. A small port is set between rocks, and a natural swimming pool is hidden among the black rocks. Here, unlike other *fajãs*, the underlying rock is not the product of landslide but of lava flow. A serpentine road leads down to the village, which almost has the feeling of an island in itself. It is a quite magical place to visit and explore.

Below: *At Cais do Topo, a sea-washed bathing pool is a perfect place to relax on a hot day.*

CHEESES FROM SÃO JORGE

The start of production of the **São Jorge cheese** is attributed to the Flemish in the latter part of the 15th century, and records exist from as early as 1547 showing exports of cheese to Terceira, Faial and São Miguel. The cheese has an intense flavour, which increases with maturation and size.

West of Norte Grande a road clambers over the high tableland towards Urzelina, crossing Pico das Brenhas and offering a splendid view of the numerous volcanic cones along the central part of the island, that contrast starkly with the surrounding green pastures and blue lakes. Here, as elsewhere on the island, the pastures are bounded not by walls, but by long rows of hydrangea. This is a great undulating, twisting road to travel, with endless fascination.

SETE FONTES FOREST PARK ★★

The Forest Park of the Seven Fountains is a delightful place for a picnic. Here, the forestry department has indulged in ornamental planting and introduced a small pets' corner to amuse children. This is a lovely mix of grassland and woodland, and, as most of the access roads are unsurfaced (not motorable), it makes for good walking, too. Prominent in the woodland are the Japanese cedar, and huge **ferns**, as well as a beautiful spread of **azalea**. Above the central area of the park, a dirt road leads up to a stunning **viewpoint**, **Pico da Velha**, from which to gaze down on Rosais, and across to the islands of Pico and Faial. The immediate landscape is one of patterned fields and isolated houses radiating from the tiny centre of Rosais, while you can also see along the backbone of the island.

ROSAIS ★★

This small linear village also gives its name to all the land at the end of the island, west from Velas. Many of the roads here are lined with hydrangea, which are also used as field boundaries, but there are African lily (*Agapanthus*), azalea and camellia, too, as well as the abundantly flowering belladonna lily.

PONTA DOS ROSAIS ★★

There is more good walking to be had at the western end of the island, leading out to Ponta dos Rosais. The sea cliffs and offshore sea stacks are an important area for migrating birds, justifying the status of the area as a Site of Community Importance. The lighthouse, **Farol dos Rosais**, was abandoned after the 1980 earthquake.

São Jorge at a Glance

SATA Air Açores fly to São Jorge from Terceira, which acts as a hub. The number of daily flights changes with the season, but generally is never less than two even in winter. It is possible to get a **ferry** to São Jorge from Terceira, Graciosa, Pico and Faial. Times are variable according to the season, with the timetable changing at the end of May and mid-September, but the latest information is available through www.transmacor.pt In São Jorge you buy tickets from the Transmaçor office on the quayside. If you have baggage then, as you board the vessel, crew will place it in a large container which is then winched aboard, and the practice reversed when you get to where you are going. It is all very fast and efficient.

The roads are in the main of a high standard and local traffic light, although there is a fair amount of slow-moving farm traffic. So, it is worth considering picking up a rental car at the airport on arrival (but pre-book it first). Otherwise, the best way to get around is to use taxis, which are inexpensive, or to book a taxi for a day tour of the island.

There is just one hotel on São Jorge, but there are also a number of guesthouses.

São Jorge Garden Hotel, Rua Machado Pires, 9800-526 Velas, tel: 295 430 100, www.hotelsjgarden.com Quite an up-market place, but it has no restaurant. Swimming pool, bar, free Internet access in foyer, and close to the centre of town. Excellent view.

Guesthouse Jardim do Triângulo, Terreiros 91, 9800-052 Velas, tel/fax: 295 414 055, www.ecotriangulo.com Not exactly a guesthouse but rather a group of independent small cottages, little more than bedroom and bathroom in the case of four of them, plus one studio with kitchenette. Set in a palmy garden producing fruit and vegetables. Basically, bed and breakfast with a twist.

Camping

There are camp sites at Urzelina, Velas and Calheta.

The number of small restaurants and bar-cafés on São Jorge is a variable thing; new ones come, old ones go.

Restaurant Açor, Largo da Matriz 41, 9800-551 Velas, tel: 295 412 362. Speedy, friendly service in this small restaurant opposite the church. Rather more international cuisine than some other restaurants, mainly Italian.

Clube Naval, in the harbour, tel: 295 412 945. Right on the quayside, an excellent place for seafood and fresh fish. Interior decorated very much on a nautical theme.

Os Amigos Café Restaurant, Ponta de São Lourenço, 9850 Calheta , tel: 295 416 421. A friendly small bar-cum-café-cum-restaurant doing a brisk trade in mainstream Azorean dishes; lunch has an excellent buffet, dishes of the day and à la carte menu.

São Jorge is an excellent island to explore on foot, and the tourist board has developed four walking trails, with more on the way. Leaflets with maps and directions in English and Portuguese are available from the tourist office in São Jorge. All the walks are waymarked.

There are a number of small shops in the centre of Velas, and a large supermarket. Loom-woven fabrics and household items are on sale at the Cooperativa de Artesanato Senhora da Encarnação (Ribeira do Nabo, Urzelina, tel: 094 414 296). Since you can poke your head into the adjacent workroom and watch the women working at the looms or hand stitching material, you can be sure that all of the many items on sale have been made on São Jorge.

Tourist Office
São Jorge: Rua Conselheiro Dr José Pereira 3 R/C, 9800-530 Velas, tel: 295 412 440, fax: 295 412 491.

7
Pico

Exploring Pico is to discover a delightful world of secret places, a place of contrasts between the barren slopes of the massive old volcano at the heart of the island and the lush green, flowery parishes overlooking the sea. This island is exquisite, with a shoreline that is fascinating and an interior that can be rather desolate and forbidding. There is no principal centre, just three centuries-old villages – Lajes, São Roque and Madalena – and all three have a legacy of art and history, of whaling and industrious farming. The mountain, **Pico**, is *the* significant feature of the island, at 2351m (7713ft) the highest point in all of Portugal, a volcanic cone that is often seen only in glimpses through the clouds, and certainly best viewed from afar.

Technically, the island of Pico is a volcano on which the cone of Pico stands. Recent volcanic activity is identifiable in the form of the quaintly named *mistérios* (mysteries), essentially lava flows that occurred after the island had been settled and which destroyed some of the cultivated areas. Because sufficient soil cover has not yet formed it is not possible to farm these areas, and the result is a series of weird landscapes where lichen-covered rocks contrast with dense, luxuriant vegetation. The most recent of the *mistérios* dates from 1720 in Silveira, with others two years earlier at São João, Santa Luzia and Bandeiras; a much older *mistério*, formed in 1572, can be seen at Praínha do Norte.

The island was first settled in 1460, and, as with the other islands, the original economy was founded on the

DON'T MISS

*** World Heritage Site:
a remarkable pattern of spaced-out, long linear walls.
*** The ascent of Pico: only for the experienced walker.
** The Lake District: a vast nature reserve, dominated by numerous volcanic vents and lakes.
** Areia Larga: see the summer residences where wine is produced, and locate the massive pyramidal mounds of lava stones called *maroiços*.
* São Roque do Pico: a pretty town that grew wealthy as a whaling centre, and its harbour – Cais do Pico – possesses the only whaling factory.

Opposite: *Quaint village church, Pico.*

cultivation of cereals, woad for dyeing, and wine production. Life for the early settlers was difficult; they had to clear dense forest, cultivate unyielding volcanic land and build houses. Moreover, volcanic eruptions were a feature of life in the 18th century, and a constant threat. At the end of the 18th century, whaling grew in importance, and became a major activity for the islanders.

Present-day Pico has increased in prosperity made possible by the building of new ports and the airport, the re-establishment of wine production, along with cattle rearing, cheese production and fishing. Now tourism is helping to play a part, especially that form of tourism that revels in nature and exploration of the natural world. However, there are no sandy beaches on Pico, although there are many natural swimming pools, refreshed constantly by sea water; warmed by the Gulf Stream, the water is surprisingly warm.

MADALENA **

The busy town of Madalena probably thinks of itself as the capital of Pico; it has developed around a small cove that offers a mooring place for the boats that cross between

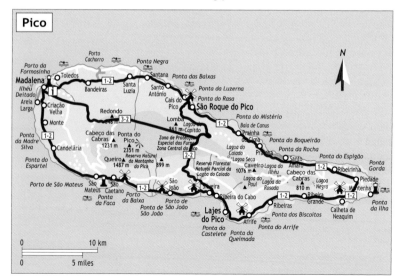

Faial and São Jorge. For centuries, cheese, wine and fruit flowed through the port of Madalena to Faial, a trade to which the town owes its economic existence.

Opposite the town, out at sea, are two large stacks, the tips of a volcanic crater; they are the islands of **Deitado** (lying down) and **Em Pé** (standing up) for fairly obvious reasons when you look at them. Today they provide shelter for sea birds, as well as giving cross-channel ferries something to aim at on the way back from Horta.

Unavoidable to the eye as you head into Madalena is the **Church of Santa Maria Madalena**, which dates from the 17th century and is the island's largest church. Around the church, the streets are a pleasure to wander; life is calm, nothing is hurried.

Areia Larga **

South of Madalena along the coast is **Areia Larga**, a village that has a small port used as an alternative to Madalena during bad weather. During the 18th and 19th centuries, summer residences were built in Areia Larga for the owners of the vineyards. What cannot be supposed is that the creation of vineyards was an easy matter. Among the vines there are huge pyramidal mounds of lava stones called *maroiços*, which are, in effect, clearance cairns dating from the time when the land was nothing but lava boulder fields requiring arduous, back-breaking clearance. Such is their place in history that these piles of volcanic debris are specially protected.

If these pyramidal piles tell of prodigious effort to clear areas for planting, then the innumerable stone walls surrounding Pico's prized vineyards surely challenge for the award of man's greatest endeavour. One estimate suggests that laid end-to-end the walls on Pico alone would easily go round the world. Each vineyard is surrounded by a thick wall, higher than a man, in order to withstand the winds of winter. Within the vineyards some measuring one 'moio' (an ancient unit of measurement equivalent to 60,000m^2), the walled areas were subdivided into plots of around 20ha (50 acres) separated by partitions. Each of these was further subdivided by parallel walls 2 or 3m (6.5

A Taste of Pico

Octopus stew: prepared in the local *vinho de cheiro* wine, octopus stew is the most typical dish of Pico. Pico's own cheese is also a great favourite, slightly flattened with a yellow rind, soft inside and a lovely aroma. For something a little more exotic try **fried moray eel with sweet potato and pickle** (*Moreia frita com batata-doce e curtume*): After marinating the eel in wine and garlic for 24 hours, it is covered with cornflour, fried in oil and served with *curtume*, a pickle made from *perrexil*, a seaside plant.

PICO WINE

The vines grown on the lava fields of Pico near Madalena produce a wine from a grape variety known as *verdelho*. It has been a justly celebrated drink for more than 200 years and probably longer, being particularly appreciated in England, America and Russia, where, perhaps surprisingly, the tsars acquired quite a taste for it. During the 19th century, the vines were attacked by mildew and phylloxera, which decimated the vineyards. As the land on which the vine had been planted was unsuitable for growing other crops, an American grape variety, Isabella, was introduced. Today the vineyards are flourishing again and producing a light and scented low alcohol wine – *vinho do cheiro* – that is the perfect accompaniment to fish dishes on warm evenings. Other varieties of wine are also available these days, notably the white *Terras da Lava* and the red *Basalto*.

or 10ft) high into 'corrals'. The ingenuity that figured all this out is quite remarkable, the key aim being to prevent the wind from circulating without shutting out sunlight. The system visually looks a mess (except from the air, when it looks fabulous), but it certainly works. The resultant stone network is a testimony to long-dead heroes, hard-working men drawn from what in those days was a tiny population (*see* 'World Heritage Site', page 96).

Areia Larga is the headquarters of the **Cooperativa Vitivinicola** that produces Pico's wines. The centre is open to visitors on weekdays at variable times.

On the other side of Madalena is another story linked with wine production, one that continues to this day. Here, along the coast, as at Areia Larga, are a number of **adegas**, or manor houses, although manor house is too grandiose a term for this motley collection of austere, huddled, stone-built single-storey houses in which the wine-producing landowners live during the summer months, until the harvest is gathered in. They make a forlorn sight in winter when the owners have retreated to warmer, more palatial residences. But they represent a very close link to the way of life here, and are part of a thread that reaches far back into the history of these islands.

Right: *A traditional wine-producing adega at Areia Larga.*

Criação Velha

This village marks the start of the area where vines are grown in the dark soil of the open holes in the slabs (*lajes*) of lava, and are known as '**Lajido**' wines.

São Mateus

Ravaged by volcanoes in 1572 and 1718, the village of São Mateus was one of the first areas of Pico to be settled, in 1482, and the place from which whaling boats set out in search of their quarry.

São João

This lovely village is an important cheese-producing centre, and has a white church perched on black rocks.

Lajes do Pico

Windmills beside the road are a feature of the **Silveira Forest Park**, which precedes the road to **Lajes do Pico**. This sleepy little village is where the first settlers came ashore, attracted by the sheltered cove. The three former boathouses that comprise the **Whaling Museum** are all that remain to tell that Lajes was once a major centre of the whaling industry that flourished in the Azores for two centuries, until as recently as 1980. Open: May–September, Tuesday–Friday 09:30–12:30, 14:00–17:30, weekends 14:00–17:30; October–April, Tuesday–Friday 10:00–12:30, 14:00–17:00, weekends 14:00–15:30. Closed Mondays and public holidays.

The Lake District **

The central-eastern part of Pico is a vast nature reserve, dominated by numerous volcanic vents and lakes that are all worth seeking out. Locating (the) **Lagoa do Caiado**, (the) **Lagoa Seca** and (the) **Lagoa do Paul** leads through some of the finest vegetated areas in the Azores, and is an excellent introduction to the natural history of the island. The mountain of Pico, of course, overshadows the landscape, but further east it is the smaller cones that take precedence and provide an intimate and invigorating scene. Up here cattle often graze, and it is not unusual to see a few of the **cows** hobbled by awkward-looking blocks

Right: *Monumental reminder of the island's dependency in the past on whaling: São Roque do Pico.*

of wood. These cows are leaders of the herd around whom the rest of the cattle gather, and by preventing them from walking quickly, or for that matter comfortably, the herd is effectively confined to a manageable area.

São Roque do Pico *

This pretty town grew wealthy as a whaling centre, and its harbour – **Cais do Pico** – possesses the island's only whaling factory, which opened in the 1940s and closed in 1981 (**Fábrica da Baleira**). The factory has now been converted to a whaling museum displaying the technology used in turning whales into oil and meat. Open: May–September, Tuesday–Friday 09:00–19:00, weekends and public holidays 09:00–17:00; October–April, 09:00–16:00 daily, except Mondays.

Santa Luzia *

The white church tower rises above the houses in this traditional wine-producing area in which vines grow in pockets of soil surrounded by black stone walls.

Porto Cachorro

Not far from the airport, the tiny village of Porto Cachorro would be largely unnoticed but for the configuration of a piece of coastal lava that resembles a small dog – which is what *cachorro* means.

WHALING

Portugal only stopped hunting whales in 1987; today they are 'hunted' for more gentle reasons – to please tourists. But for over 150 years, with backbone, oars, courage and daring, harpoons and the ancient techniques employed by whale hunters across the world, the whale hunters of the Azores came to leave an indelible mark on the landscape, the architecture and the musical traditions of these islands. Much of this legacy is explained in the whaling museum at Lajes do Pico.

The Ascent of Pico: 2351m (7713ft)

Looked on as one of the world's most shapely volcanoes, the symmetrical profile of Pico is inviting and gives the impression that it is easy to climb. That is true up to a roundabout, to which a road leads, at **Cabeço das Cabras**, at 1231m (4039ft). Beyond this point requires a good deal of experience; it is not a simple walk. A good level of fitness is needed, along with suitable footwear and adequate clothing, and, if the weather is variable, the services of a guide. A list of 40 mountain guides is available at the tourist office. A warden from the Fire Services holds station at the upper end of the motorable road, and walkers are required to sign in, and sign out on their return. The ascent and descent takes around four hours, plus an extra hour if Piquinho is included. During the day, in good conditions, the path is easy to follow, and involves a little scrambling. The top of the mountain is quite barren.

On the way up, the route passes **Furna**, a cavern within the volcanic cone. The central crater of Pico, called **Pico Grande**, is monumentally impressive, a tortured landscape with a diameter of around 700m (2300ft). From within this crater arises **Piquinho** (**Pico Pequeno**), a volcanic cone standing 50m (165ft) above the rim of the main crater, and

Below: *The symmetrical cone of Pico, Portugal's highest summit, probes a layer of clouds, seen from the neighbouring island of São Jorge.*

Right: *Lava formations, looking across to São Jorge from Areia Larga.*

the true summit. Fumaroles on Piquinho emit a strong sulphurous smell as a reminder that volcanoes are seldom truly dormant. Many mountaineers climb Pico during the night to see the sunrise, and claim that it is one of the most memorable experiences.

World Heritage Site ★★★

The 987ha (240-acre) World Heritage Site on Pico consists of a remarkable pattern of spaced-out, long linear walls running inland from, and parallel to, the rocky shore. Evidence of this viniculture, whose origins date back to the 15th century, is manifest in the extraordinary assembly of the fields, in houses and early 19th-century manor houses, in wine-cellars, churches and ports. The exceptionally beautiful man-made landscape of the site is the best remaining area of a once much more widespread practice.

This landscape reflects a unique response to viniculture on a small volcanic island and one that has been evolving since the arrival of the first settlers in the 15th century. The exceptional man-made terrain of small, stone-walled fields is testimony to generations of small-scale farmers who, in a hostile environment, created a sustainable living and much-prized wine. It is for this reason that this area is designated a World Heritage Site.

Pico at a Glance

There are regular flights to Pico via Terceira. You can also use ferries either from São Jorge (Velas: around 1 hour) or Faial (Horta: 30 minutes).

There is much to be said for either hiring a car or taking a taxi. The roads on Pico are generally good around the edges and less good in the interior. Your own car allows you to drive off into unexpected turnings, but if you get the right taxi driver they are going to do this anyway. There are more than 10 taxi drivers on Pico who speak English and one who speaks French; most taxi drivers somehow manage to communicate very well in a mix of languages. They have organized themselves into a small consortium (**Associação Taxistas da Ilha do Pico**) and collectively offer four different tours of the island depending on your availability. One at least of the hotels also offers island tours. These are a little more expensive than a taxi for the day, although they may well include a picnic lunch, whereas with a taxi driver you may well (but not necessarily) find yourself buying his/her lunch.

Aldeia da Fonte, Caminho da Fonte/Silveira, 9930-117 Lajes do Pico, tel: 292 679 500, www.aldeiadafonte.com

Not what you might regard as a conventional hotel, and while the luxury you might expect is here, the emphasis is about appreciation of nature, relaxation, environmentally friendly attitudes, and 'getting away from it all'. Quite different.

Hotel Caravelas, Rua Conselheiro Terra Pinheiro 3, 9950-329 Madalena, Pico, tel: 292 628 550, www.hotel caravelas.net A short walk from the ferry port. Has 67 rooms equipped with telephone, TV; bar, solarium and swimming pool.

Pico Hotel, Rua dos Biscoitos, 9950-334 Madalena, tel: 292 628 400, www.picohotel.com Has 69 rooms, restaurant in black rock with terrace and bar, outdoor swimming pool, garden, health club and sauna, Turkish bath and Jacuzzi.

Miradouro-da-Papalva Inn, Ramal Salazar 13, São João, 9930-427 Lajes, tel/fax: 292 673 006, www.miradouro-da-papalva.com Small 'residencial' away from the ferry port; English and Portuguese spoken.

Espaço Talassa Lodge, Lajes do Pico, tel: 292 672 010, www.espacotalassa.com Offering 12 rooms and close to the whale watching facility, the lodge is ideal for visitors with a keen interest in whale and dolphin watching, permitting a longer stay.

Camping
There are camp sites at Lajes do Pico and Santo António.

There are a number of small bar-restaurants in Madalena, but the best place to eat on the island is the **Hocus Pocus Restaurant** (tel: 292 679 504) in the Hotel Aldeia da Fonte.

Ancoradouro Restaurante, Areia Larga, 9950-302 Madalena, tel: 292 623 490. Serves the speciality 'fish stew', along with other fish courses, meat and regional cuisine.

Aguascristalinas Restaurante, Rua das Poças, 9940-230 São Roque do Pico, tel: 292 648 230. Specializing in regional cuisine, and a wide range of fish and seafood dishes.

Whale Watching
Espaço Talassa, Rua do Saco, 9930 Lajes do Pico, tel: 292 672 010, fax: 292 672 617, www.espacotalassa.com Tours depart from Lajes do Pico daily at 10:00 and 15:00, and the fee includes a 30-minute briefing, a 3-hour sea-going excursion, a visit to the nearby whaling museum and to the Queimada Lookout Post.

Walking
Away from the central mountain, Pico is a remarkable island to explore on foot, and the tourist board has developed a number of walking trails.

Tourist Office
Gare Maritima da Madalena, 9950 Madalena, Pico, tel/fax: 292 623 524.

8
Faial

To see Faial in the spring and early summer when the field hedgerows of hydrangea are in bloom immediately illustrates why Faial is known as '**The Blue Island**'. The sight is amazing; whole hillsides are awash with blues and greens as the hedgerows clash with the meadows and produce grown within. Along with other islands in the Azores archipelago, the island is of volcanic origin and is close to the tectonic divide between the European and American plates. Indeed, the island might be considered the westernmost point of Europe (the two islands further west, Flores and Corvo, are on the American plate). Relatively small in size in comparison to Pico, the centre of the island is dominated by **Cabeço Gordo** and its *caldeira*.

The 30-minute **ferry ride** from Madalena on Pico is the best way to approach Faial, offering as it does a lovely retrospect of Pico and the anticipation of a new island as the boat pulls into the harbour in Horta. For certain, the pulse of Faial is in Horta, the main town and harbour. Elsewhere the island is dotted with attractive villages and beaches, notably at Porto Pim, Praia do Almoxarife and Praia da Fajã.

The road that circles the island from Horta offers a splendid way to gain an impression of the island, a place where river valleys separate small communities from each other: Praia do Almoxarife and Pedro Miguel north of Horta are two such settlements. As the road heads northwest it arrives at **Ribeirinha** where pastures sheltered by a ridge covered with rich vegetation give the district a beguiling beauty. **Salão** brings lovely vistas of fields hedged by hydrangeas, and, a few kilometres further, almost at the

Corvo
● Vila do Corvo
● Lajes das Flores   *Graciosa*
Flores   ●Santa Cruz da Graciosa
            São Jorge   *Terceira*
       ●Velas ●●Praia da Vitória
Faial   Angra do Heroísmo
  Horta   *Pico*   *São Miguel*
       Lajes
       do Pico
                Ponta Delgada
ATLANTIC   Santa Maria ●
OCEAN   Vila do
                          Porto

DON'T MISS

*** **The Capelinhos volcano:** a moving and memorable sight.
** **The Scrimshaw Museum:** contains hundreds of sperm whale teeth worked with scrimshaw.
** **Horta Museum:** the largest museum in the Azores.
** **Monte da Guia:** this shapely mound is the cone of a former volcano, and offers an excellent view over Horta.
** **Caldeira:** an impressive bowl of lush green vegetation.

Opposite: *The style of windmills vary from island to island: Faial has a distinctive four-sailed version built on a solid stone foundation.*

northern tip of the island, is **Cedros**, a village believed to be the oldest settlement on the island. Beyond Cedros, the ocean cliff slopes become steeper near the west coast communities of Praia do Norte, from where there are fine views over Fajã. The volcanic black lava and deep vegetation continues in the areas around Fajã da Praia do Norte and Norte Pequeno. After that Capelo is reached, and the volcanic story that is Capelinhos (see page 106).

The original name of Faial was *Insula de La Ventura* (Venture Island), and it was discovered in 1427 by Diogo de Silves while in the service of the king of Portugal. The island's first inhabitant is said to be a hermit. He was followed by Josse van Huertere, who came ashore at Praia de Almofariz (now Praia do Almoxarife) in the east of the island. His unsuccessful quest to Faial was to look for tin and silver. But in 1468 van Huertere became the donee-captain and gained consent from the king to settle the island with his Flemish countrymen. The island is named after him. As with

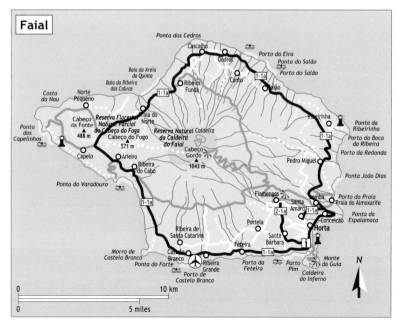

Left: *The farmland of Faial is especially lush, the fields typically bordered either by hydrangea or bamboo.*

the other islands, farming and the cultivation of plants for the dyeing process brought a measure of prosperity, although trade did not significantly develop until the 19th century, when the safety of the harbour at Horta gained renown.

HORTA ★★

In Horta marina there are yachts from all over the world. The crews linger in the bars, enjoying the atmosphere of Faial and bringing a cosmopolitan feel to the town. Horta has been frequented by yachts since the early 19th century when *Cleopatra's Barge* tied up at the port during a cruise. Others followed, including Joshua Slocum (who made the first solo voyage round the world), Sir Francis Chichester and Eric Tabarly. The opening of the marina in 1986 enlarged the port's capacity, and enhanced Horta's already legendary nautical and sporting tradition. Today, the *frisson* of excitement, the sense of having reached a charismatic destination, is almost tangible from the moment of arrival.

Horta's streets are lined with ancient buildings, many associated with transatlantic cable companies. In the contorted streets and cobbled alleyways whitewashed houses, attractive town squares and colourful gardens harmonize with the imposing façades of churches, bell towers and museums displaying rustic art carved in whalebone and fig.

A TASTE OF FAIAL

Faial Island roast beans (*Feijão assado*): Previously stewed with *linguiça* and pork rashers, the beans are kept with their sauce and returned to the oven to cook further. This is a dish of the people, based on beans, to which the pork is added just to introduce additional flavour. Local knowledge about conservation methods resulted in the creation of many varieties of this dish, and it is common to add sugar, cinnamon and sugar cane syrup. These extra ingredients, linked to the use of clay pots for storage and the surface layer of fat that congealed on the stew when it had cooled, made this an easy dish to transport, and it was often consumed on the big American whaling ships.

GRAFFITI ART

Covering every inch of the marina's walls and walkways are painted inscriptions of past visitors – a kind of 'yachtie graffiti' graphically portraying global wanderings. Many are simple maps tracing trans-Atlantic or round-the-world routes, but at the centre of each are the Azores. Lines drawn from Cape Town, Southampton, New York and Buenos Aires all converge on this tiny archipelago.

Located between two bays, sheltered by two dormant volcanoes, and divided by the isthmus leading to Monte da Guia, Horta is expanding, and already stretches along a bay that is one of the rare sheltered anchorages in the Azores. Since 1976, Horta has been the seat of the Parliament of the Autonomous Region of the Azores, as well as headquarters for many of the administrative bodies.

The 18th-century **clock tower** is all that remains of the former parish church of Horta, built in the 16th century, and destroyed by earthquake, finally being demolished in 1825. In Rua Vasco da Gama, a three-storey 19th-century building inscribed **Sociedade de Carvão e Fornecimentos do Fayal** is a link with the times past when Horta was a vital supply centre for the steam ships crossing the Atlantic. A short way further down the street, the house at **No. 28**, also 19th century, is Art Nouveau (*arte nova*) in style, and has an interesting glass-encased balcony. The harbour walls, as is tradition, bear paintings done by yachtsmen over the years in thanksgiving for a safe cross-

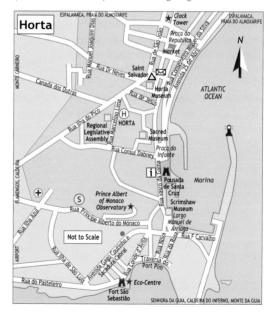

ing of the ocean. The sea wall was constructed in 1876, and gives an interesting view of the town.

Horta Museum is the largest museum in the Azores, and houses a number of temporary exhibitions and a room displaying works executed in fig tree pith and fish scales by a Faial artist, Euclides Rosa. The museum as a whole contains a wide range of eclectic material of a global nature but of relevance to Faial. Open: October–April, Tuesday–Friday 10:00–12:00, 14:00–17:00, weekends 14:00–17:30; May–September, Tuesday–Friday 09:30–12:30, 14:00–17:30, weekends 14:00–17:30. Admission to the museum also includes admission to the Capelhinos Exhibition (see page 107), but such a combined ticket is valid only for one day.

The Scrimshaw Museum accessed via **Peter Café Sport** contains hundreds of sperm whale teeth worked with scrimshaw (see page 13), along with books of dedications and other mementoes of visiting yachtspeople. Open: Monday–Saturday 09:30–13:00, 14:00–18:30, Sunday 09:00–13:00 and 16:00–18:30 (Sunday, October–March, 09:00–13:00).

The café itself is something of an institution, and can trace its history back to 1901 when local-born **Ernesto Ávila Azevedo** founded **Casa Açoreana**, a place where people could buy drinks as well as the handicrafts for which he was renowned. The original *casa* was situated

Above: *A colourful rainbow over Horta, seen from Monte da Guia.*

FIG PITH AND FISH SCALES

The handicrafts produced on Faial use some unusual materials: flowers are made from fish scales, and translucent figures made from the pith of fig trees. There are many examples of this amazing skill in Horta Museum, as well as embroidery and crochet. It is thought that this unusual art originated in convent cloisters at the hands of nuns.

Above: *Peter Café Sport and the Scrimshaw Museum, Faial.*

next to the port in the same place as today's café, which came into being as Café Sport in 1918 and has retained the same bluish colouring ever since. Over the years the café became a place of refuge and assistance for sailors crossing the ocean, and remains so today; its bustling, fuggy, chatty atmosphere, coffee machines hissing frantically, and the chance to buy souvenirs next door, is a good reason for finding time in Horta to take a quick coffee in this historical establishment.

MONTE DA GUIA **

This shapely mound is the cone of a former volcano, and offers an excellent view over Horta, the beach and bay of Porto Pim, the rest of Faial and across the sea to Pico and beyond. There is also a view of **Caldeira do Inferno**, a former crater now filled by the sea. Near the summit is a **Fisherman's Chapel**, built in the 17th century, but moved to its present position when changes were made for the defence of Horta during World War II. On the isthmus linking Horta with Monte da Guia is the **Casa dos Cabos**, the place where the cables laid in 1923 and 1928 were secured.

CONCEIÇÃO *

The village of Conceição nestles in a valley, and nearby, housed in the former Quinta de São Lourenço, with its 17th-century manor house and chapel, are the **botanic gardens**, displaying plants from the archipelago and wider across Macronesia. Open: mid-June to mid-October, Monday–Friday 09:30–17:00, weekends 14:00–17:30; mid-October to mid-June, Monday–Friday 09:00–12:30, 14:00–17:00.

Ponta da Espalamaca is a steep cliff overlooking the town, and from a *miradouro* next to a religious monument there is an excellent **view** not only of Horta, but of the islands of Pico, São Jorge and Graciosa, and the immediate **Flamengos** with its many plantations, flowers and cottages. This is a good place, too, to observe that while other parts of the island use hydrangeas as hedgerow material, here they prefer bamboo.

From the viewpoint a road passes attractive **windmills** and then wends upwards to the rim of the *caldeira*, an impressive bowl of lush green vegetation – cedars, ferns, juniper, mosses and hydrangea. From the road end, a tunnel leads through the rim of the crater to a spectacular viewpoint. There is what remains of a lake at the bottom of the *caldeira*, and its outline can clearly be seen, but this largely dried up during the Capelinhos eruption. Equally enthralling is a stepped path that leads from the road end up to a slightly higher vantage point.

> ### HYDRANGEAS
>
> The islands of the Azores are covered with them, and in many places they are used as hedgerows with dazzling effect in spring and early summer. Originally, hydrangeas were imported from China and Japan, and have flourished in the climate of the Azores. But, for some reason, Faial, the 'Blue Island', seems to have more than its fair share, not only edging meadows, but framing houses and farm buildings, lining roadsides and generally enamelling the countryside with exuberant colour.

Left: *The Fisherman's chapel on Monte da Guia proves to be a superb viewpoint overlooking the main town of Horta.*

WALKING THE RIM

The *caldeira* is 2km (1 mile) in diameter, 400m (1312ft) deep and has a perimeter (walkable) of 7km (4 miles), rising to the high point of the island, **Cabeço Gordo**, at 1043m (3421ft). A round-trip walk of 45–60 minutes from the road-end car park should be enough to visit Cabeço Gordo, while the complete circuit of the crater rim should take between two and three hours.

CEDROS

This tiny village, thought to have been the first place to have been settled, lost its Gothic church in a fire and only a bell tower now remains. There is a small **museum** here, in a traditional-style house, featuring furniture and agricultural tools. Open: Monday–Friday 09:00–12:30, 14:30–17:30.

THE CAPELINHOS VOLCANO ★★★

The landscape around the site of the Capelinhos Volcano is unbelievable: a dark, austere, forbidding scene of volcanic destruction, and yet a place of immense importance in the study of vulcanology.

Following the principal volcanic activity responsible for the creation of Faial, over the centuries there have been secondary eruptions, adding to the backbone of the island. The Capelinhos volcano was the most recent of these, active from 1957 to 1958, and is the youngest volcanic cone of the Capelo Peninsula, a region made up of 20 or so cones and related lava flows. On the morning of 27 September 1957, around 08:00, a submarine eruption about 1km (0.6 mile) from the westernmost point of Faial was preceded between 16 and 27 September by seismic activity during which over 200 earthquakes were experienced by the people of the island. The volcanic activity passed through a number of phases, from the emission of gases to violent explosions and

Below: *A recent addition: the Ponta dos Capelinhos is the newest appendage to the Azorean islands, and the result of volcanic activity in 1957.*

jets of black ash that reached heights of over 1000m (3280ft), overtopped by clouds of water vapour that reached even higher, and throwing incandescent lava up to 500m (1640ft) into the air. By 10 October, the volcanic output had already formed a small island, but this had sunk into the sea by the end of the month. Then, at the beginning of November, eruptions began again and a new island was formed which by 12 November was connected to Faial by an isthmus.

Compared with other underwater eruptions that are a feature of the Azores archipelago, the eruptions at Capelinhos were of unusually long duration. Capelinhos ended only on 24 October 1958, over a year after it began, having ejected over 30 million tons of lava and ash.

When, finally, all the eruptions ceased, not only had Faial grown in size by about 2.4km² (1 sq mile), but around 300 houses were totally buried beneath volcanic ash – you can today see the tops of their red-tiled roofs poking through the ash layers. Following the devastation, then Senator John F Kennedy from Massachusetts (later President Kennedy) and Senator John O Pastore from Rhode Island proposed special legislation to allow people from the Azores who had been impacted by the volcano to immigrate to the United States of America. More than 2000 people were made homeless, and many of those who had lost their houses and farming land accepted the invitation, and left the island for America.

The nearby lighthouse, one of the older designs in the Azores, was almost completely buried beneath ash, but has since been 'released' and is now the focus of a restoration project on the dramatic volcanic episodes of the mid-1950s. For many years completely barren, the volcanic slopes are slowly being colonized by tough vegetation and lichens. Not surprisingly, the Capelinhos Volcano site is part of the Natura 2000 Network, both as a Site of Community Importance and a Special Protection Area. It is a moving experience to walk among the lava flows and across the uncompromising blanket of ash.

The story of the eruption is told in the **Capelinhos Volcano Exhibition** which is situated in an old, rectangular traditional stone house (*atafona*), although ongoing restora-

DESTRUCTION

Touring round the island you'll see numerous desolate buildings, destroyed by the earthquake in 1998, and left abandoned; others, with just the tops of their roofs showing, lie buried beneath volcanic ash from the 1957 eruption at Capelinhos. The 1998 earthquake on 9 July shook Faial, Pico and São Jorge and measured 5.6 on the Richter scale. It caused moderate damage to the parishes of Ribeirinha, Pedro Miguel, Salão and Cedros, but had greater impact in Castelo Branco (mainly Lombega), Flamengos and Praia do Almoxarife. Nor did the adjacent islands escape: parts of Pico and the far western part of São Jorge were also affected by the earthquake. In all, eight people lost their lives and 1700 were made homeless.

Above: *Volcanic craters (caldeiras) are a feature of all the islands, but there are few more attractive than the hydrangea-bordered caldeira on Faial.*

tion work at the lighthouse suggests that the location of the exhibition may change in future years. It contains numerous photographs and press cuttings from the time, giving first-hand accounts of the devastation. There is also a display of material projected from the volcano during the eruption – lava samples and 'bombs'. Open: May–September, Tuesday–Friday 09:30–12:30, 14:00–17:30, weekends 14:00–17:30; October–April, Tuesday–Friday 10:00–noon, 14:00–17:00, weekends 14:00–17:00. Closed Mondays and public holidays. The Capelhinos Museological Nucleus is part of the Museum of Horta, and one ticket gains admission to both sites, but is valid only for one day.

Morro de Castelo Branco ★★

Not yet an island, but destined to become one in time, Morro de Castelo Branco, just west of the airport, is a fascinating piece of vulcanology. The lava that flowed from the volcanic eruption here was highly viscous and did not run freely, and solidified into a cohesive cone, almost cylindrical in form. Gradually it has become eroded, leaving the top of a lava column exposed. One day it will become an island; much, much later it will collapse and disappear altogether, and the many sea birds that find this a perfect habitat will have to find a new home.

Faial at a Glance

WHERE TO STAY

Faial Resort Hotel, Rua Cônsul Dabney, 9901-856 Horta, tel: 292 207 400, www.fayalhotel.com Quite central to Horta, and about 10km (6 miles) from the airport; good view over Horta and across to Pico. Has 125 rooms and six suites, fully equipped. Restaurant, bars, swimming pool, Jacuzzi, sauna, gymnasium, laundry.

Hotel do Canal, Largo Dr Manual de Arriaga, 9900-026 Horta, tel: 292 202 120. Within walking distance of the ferry port, the Hotel do Canal is popular. The ocean motifs in the hotel's interior tell the history of this island, where tradition holds that there should always be a safe port. Has 103 rooms, restaurant, bar, Jacuzzi, sauna, gymnasium, laundry.

Pousada de Santa Cruz, Rua Vasco da Gama, 9900-144 Horta, tel: 292 202 200, www.pousadas.pt Pousadas are up-market guesthouses and have been a feature of Portuguese hospitality for over 50 years. There is just one on Faial; this one. The guesthouse is set in a 16th-century fortress built over Horta Bay and classified as a National Monument since 1947. Excellent view of Pico and the harbour.

Casa do Capitão (Rural Tourism), Rua do Capitão 5, 9900-341 Cedros, tel/fax: 292 946 121, www.casado capitao.net Located in Cedros,

a rural 'Faialense' town about 17km (10 miles) from Horta (the main city on the island), the Casa do Capitão is a peaceful oasis surrounded by small houses built of volcanic stone, cultivated fields, pastures and back yards lined with fruit trees. The house has traditional architecture with a stone-inlay façade and a small landscaped 'patio' at the centre, ideal for a breakfast or a late afternoon tea. There are several paths that meander from the house into the countryside or along the coast with distant views of São Jorge and Graciosa islands.

WHERE TO EAT

A full list of all restaurants on the island is available from the tourist office. Here are just a few:

Medalhas Taberan and Casa de Pasto, Rua de Serpa Pinto 22, 9900-095 Horta, tel: 292 391 026. A rustic eatery serving Azorean cuisine – spicy sausage, blood sausage, boneless rib-eye steak, blue jack mackerel and yams – in a lovely and basic setting. Typical Azorean cuisine.

Restaurante O Kapote, Av. Marginal, Horta, tel: 917 951 452. Basic Azorean specialities, self-service buffet, and music. The place for fresh fish.

Canto da Roca, Rua Nova, tel: 292 292 444. Specializes in home-cooked food, very much the traditional food of the islands.

Peter Café Sport, Rua José Azevedo 9, 9900 Horta, tel: 292 392 897, www.peter cafesport.com No visit to Faial is complete without at least taking coffee in this long-established and industrious bar, founded in 1918; don't expect to find a free seat, just stand by the bar and take it all in. If taking lunch, get there early. This is a meeting place for yachtsmen and women from all over the world.

TOURS AND EXCURSIONS

Whale and Dolphin Watching
Whale Watching Peter, Rua José Azevedo 9, 9900 Horta, tel: 292 392 897, www.petercafesport.com

WALKING

Faial is a perfect island to explore on foot, and the tourist board has developed a number of walking trails. Excellent leaflets with maps and directions in English and Portuguese are available from the tourist office in Madalena; all the walks are clearly way-marked.

USEFUL CONTACTS

Regional Directorate of Tourism of the Azores Rua Comendador Ernesto Rebelo 14, 9900 Horta, tel: 292 200 500, fax: 292 200 501.

Tourist Office Rua Vasco da Gama, 9900-017 Horta, tel: 292 292 237, fax: 292 292 006.

9
Flores

The most scenically beautiful of the Azorean islands, Flores, like its near neighbour, Corvo, lies far out in the Atlantic, with the warmth of the Gulf Stream and a (generally) mild maritime climate producing perfect conditions to bring the island into bloom every year, earning it the epithet, 'The Island of Flowers'. This is an island of spectacular beauty, and the one island everyone should include in a visit to the Azores.

Flores represents the **western edge of Europe**, even though it sits on the North American tectonic plate. The significance of the geological divide is that neither Flores nor Corvo experience earthquakes. Purists wanting to locate the actual westernmost point of Europe will have to be strong swimmers: the **Ilhéu de Monchique**, a tiny rocky islet, lies offshore across vexatious currents. Visits are not advised.

Synonymous with unspoilt nature, the island is rugged, with a dramatic **coastline** and wild and exciting landscapes of miniature mountains that are the finest in the Azores. The lush vegetation, however, indicates that there are few days in the year when rain does not fall here, but it is rarely prolonged and heavy. Visiting Flores is to take a walk with nature, visiting **waterfalls**, rivers and streams, and countless meadows bound by a network of hydrangeas.

Santa Cruz das Flores is where the airport is, seemingly from some angles, right in the centre of town; **Lajes das Flores** has a rather better port capable of accepting the container ships that bring weekly supplies to the island. Both towns have been inhabited since the 15th century.

DON'T MISS

*** The Lake District:** take a taxi ride around the island and visit the spectacular region of the lakes.
** Fajã Grande and Fajãzinha:** along the west coast, with impressive waterfalls.
** Rocha dos Bordões:** this dramatic rock rises above the main coastal road south of Mosteiro.
** Ponta Delgada:** at the northern tip of the island, with a view of Corvo.

Opposite: The island of Flores lies far out in the Atlantic, and its western coast, here at Porto da Fajã Grande, is the westernmost point of Portugal.

It is not clear when the island of Flores was discovered, but it was first known as São Tomás, and only later turned to Flores, because of the abundance of the flowers known as goldenrod. The island appears to have been settled first in around 1470, but after a few years of effort abandoned for a further 20 years before being populated from both Terceira and Madeira, and then colonists from mainland Portugal.

For decades, turning into centuries, the islands knew peace and tranquillity, disturbed only by the plundering attentions of pirates in the late 15th and early 16th centuries. The area around Flores is where privateers lay in wait for ships returning from South America laden with gold and silver.

When whaling began in the Azores, a factory was set up in Santa Cruz and, today redundant, is on the brink of restoration as a museum to the industry.

THE LAKE DISTRICT ★★★

A tour of the island breaks easily into two parts; the larger is the **centre-south** section that visits the numerous **lakes**

Flores

Left: *The interior of Flores is a landscape of lakes upon lakes: Caldeira Funda (left) and Caldeira Rasa (right).*

nestling in volcanic craters, a tour of which also takes in Lajes das Flores. The highest point of the island is **Morro Alto**, at 914m (2999ft), lying just to the north of the lakes **Lagoa Seca**, **Lagoa Branca**, **Lagoa Comprida** and **Lagoa Negra** (also called Lagoa Funda).

Morro Alto **

The centre-north area of **Morro Alto** is a Site of Community Importance, but also includes parts of the **Caldeira Funda** and **Rasa Natural Forest Reserve** to the south, as well as the entire Natural Forest Reserve of Morro Alto and Pico de Sé Partial. The whole area is lush with vegetation, and typified by medium-sized volcanic cones with steep sides. This central highland region of Flores is a wetland that is one of the oldest, best preserved and largest in the Azores. A road leads up to Morro Alto, and from here the whole island can be seen.

West Coast ***

On the west coast, **waterfalls** stream down near-vertical cliffs between **Fajã Grande** and **Fajãzinha**, approached by delightfully serpentine roads that offer stunning cameos of the coastal landscape and its villages. **Fajãzinha** is a rash

---

LAGOONS

The many lakes, or lagoons, were formed when the central chamber of a volcano collapsed, leading to slow erosion of the interior of the crater which gradually filled with water. The beauty of these lakes is nowhere better exemplified than in the almost aerial view from Mercela Hill of the **Caldeira Rasa**, a lake of blue, across the road from which, and much lower down, is the **Caldeira Funda**, a lake of eye-catching green.

of white and terracotta houses huddled inside a former volcanic *caldeira*. Overlooking it on a hill is the **Church of Nossa Senhora dos Remédios** (Our Lady of Remedies).

Fajã Grande has a small port, a popular pebble beach and a smattering of small restaurants and bars; this is the island's 'seaside' resort. The nearby waterfall and lake at its foot, the **Poço de Bacalhau**, is a perfect place for a dip; a short walk leads up from the road to the base of the waterfall. On the way you pass a small water mill that is still in use. Just to the north of Fajã Grande, perched precariously on a ledge, is **Porta da Fajã Grande**, seemingly at risk of being pushed forever into the Atlantic.

Rocha dos Bordões ★★

This dramatic rock rises above the main coastal road south of Mosteiro. These high, vertical strata look like a complex set of organ pipes, and were formed when the basalt solidified.

LAJES DAS FLORES

As well as having a deep-water harbour, Lajes has converted a Franciscan convent into the **Island of Flores Museum** which houses a collection of ceramics and agricultural implements used in traditional occupations and fishing. Open: Monday–Friday 09:00–12:30, 14:00–17:30.

Below: *Looking down on Ponta Delgada, the northernmost point of Flores.*

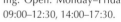

PONTA DELGADA ★★

Located at the northernmost part of the island, the village of Ponta Delgada sprawls across fertile fields bounded by a deeply indented coastline. There is a good view from here northwards to Corvo, before reaching Ponta Delgada, as the road branches left to the lighthouse (automated but manned) at **Ponta do Albarnaz**.

Flores at a Glance

GETTING THERE

SATA Air Açores fly to Flores from Ponta Delgada, Terceira and Faial, daily except Sundays.

GETTING AROUND

It is possible to hire a car on Flores and to make an independent and leisurely tour of the island. This is certainly the best option if you are likely to become mesmerized by the beauty of the landscape into just lounging around on the rim of some *caldeira*, taking it all it. But equally, there is much to be said for employing a local taxi driver to make the experience more informed; relax, let the driver take the strain. In summer, when the sea is calm, it is worth taking a boat trip round the island.

WHERE TO STAY

Servi-Flor Hotel, Antigo Bairro dos Franceses, 9970-305 Santa Cruz das Flores, tel: 292 592 453, fax: 292 592 554. A somewhat Spartan-looking hotel just a short distance from the airport (hotel pick-up), formerly belonging to a French family. The 32 rooms (and one apartment) are a reasonable size, and the food in the restaurant of a good standard, serving regional dishes. Bar, pool table, crazy golf and children's play area nearby.

Just 100m from the sea (inaccessible), and a little further from sheltered natural swimming pools.

Hotel Ocidental, Ave. dos Baleeiros, 9970-306 Santa Cruz das Flores, tel: 292 590 100, fax: 292 590 101, www.hotelocidental.com With 36 rooms, the hotel is located just 500m from the airport, and close to natural swimming pools. Many rooms have balconies and sea view. Restaurant; clean but a bit Spartan.

Pensão Residencial Vila Flores, Travessa de São José 3, 9970-341 Santa Cruz das Flores, tel: 292 592 190, fax: 292 592 621. A simple and basic guesthouse with 13 rooms in the centre of town; 50% discount for children under 10 years.

WHERE TO EAT

The choice is limited as the main hotel, **Servi-Flor**, while having a good restaurant, will only entertain non-residents in the quieter months; even so, it is worth asking at the hotel reception. The menu is traditional, favouring fish and meat. There is a small, modern bar-café not far from the Hotel Ocidental, catering mainly for people who go down to the nearby natural swimming pools.

Café-Restaurant Rosa, Rua da Conceição (near the church), tel: 292 592 162. Serves excellent seafood dishes, and is popular with the locals. To be sure of getting a table, turn up early. The Rosa arguably has the cheapest menu in town; dishes are substantial. **Restaurante Baleia**, Lugar do Boqueirao (near the old whale factory), tel: 292 592 462. Simple, unfussy food served promptly. As elsewhere, the food is predictable but wholesome.

WALKING

As with all the islands of the Azores, walking is an excellent method of exploration, and the tourist board on Flores has developed four walking trails, with more on the way. Excellent leaflets with maps and directions in English and Portuguese are available from the tourist office in Santa Cruz das Flores. All the walks are conspicuously waymarked.

USEFUL CONTACTS

Flores: Rua Dr Armas da Silveira, 9970-331 Santa Cruz das Flores, tel: 292 592 369, fax: 292 592 846. There is a small tourist information desk at the airport, with uncertain opening hours.

10
Corvo

Far from the other islands in the archipelago, even more from mainland Portugal, and actually resting on an altogether different tectonic plate, Corvo and Flores were the last islands to be discovered – by Diogo de Têves on returning from one of his trips to Terra Nova in 1452 – and Corvo the last to be inhabited.

Corvo – Crow Island – is a tiny speck of an island, the smallest island in the archipelago, the one place that many Azoreans themselves long to visit, but so few manage to do. Planning visits to Corvo is complicated by there being just a few flights each week, with the aircraft remaining on the island only briefly, leaving insufficient time to explore. Visiting Corvo really means staying on Corvo, although, weather permitting, **boat trips** operate from Flores (Santa Cruz), with the trip taking from 45 minutes to 1 hour. It is an exhilarating experience, and, arguably, the best way to get there, but with baggage it can be cumbersome.

This remote island is a **timeless and enchanting place**, as close to the traditional way of life in the Azores as it is possible to find. Its tiny, self-supporting population upholds the ancient traditions of the Azores, and life goes on at a very relaxed and nature-influenced pace. The very isolation of the island preserves its time-long ways. For centuries the only way of communicating with nearby Flores was by signal fire, with the number of fires being lit signifying whether the islanders needed a doctor, some other urgent need, or a priest.

Visitors with limited time on the island should stroll through the scant, winding streets, called *canadas*, of **Vila**

Corvo
● Vila do Corvo
● Lajes das Flores   *Graciosa*
Flores   ●Santa Cruz da Graciosa
            São Jorge   *Terceira*
      Faial ● ●Velas   ●●Praia da Vitória
         Horta Lajes *Pico* Angra do Heroísmo
            do Pico   *São Miguel*
                              ●
                          Ponta Delgada
   ATLANTIC   *Santa Maria* ●
   OCEAN   Vila do
                              Porto

DON'T MISS

*** **Monte Gordo:** choose a clear day and take a ride or walk to the summit of the island.
** **Vila do Corvo:** chill out in and around the island's only settlement.

Opposite: *Corvo is an island renowned for its cloud cover, often making excursions to its highest summit both pointless and viewless.*

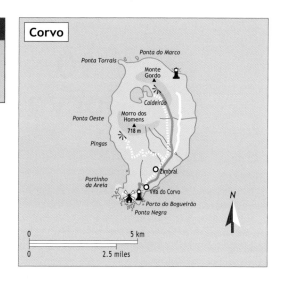

do Corvo, taking in the traditional houses with their windows framed in bright colours – the customary colours of the Azores are a white building, grey door and window lintels, and green doors and windows frames, but over the years brighter colours have been introduced.

Corvo was the last island to show the Portuguese flag, in 1452. But the first attempt to settle Corvo did not come until the 16th century, spearheaded by Antão Vaz from Terceira, who ended up abandoning the island. The same result faced the Barcelos brothers who came next. But the settlement was assured when Gonçalo de Sousa ordered some of his slaves to go to the island and graze cattle there. Somehow, they succeeded where others had failed, and were followed years later by families from nearby Flores. Over the years, the islanders of Corvo earned a reputation for courage and bravery prompting visits at the end of the 18th century of American whaling ships to recruit sailors. That same courage helped in 1632 when 10 **Algerian pirate ships** attacked the island. Armed only with farming implements, and faced with vastly superior numbers, the islanders succeeded in repelling the invasion attempt. That the islanders suffered no losses, compared with the pirates' many, was seen as a miracle and came to be revered in the parish church **Nossa Senhora dos Milágres** (Our Lady of the Miracles).

The geography includes hills with forests to the east and rocky ledges to the west and north. The town itself is located in the south of the island. Except at the southernmost part, where lava flows have created a rocky platform, the island is surrounded by tall cliffs, the tallest in the Azores. These shelter large bays with some reefs and islets which are passage points for whales, dolphins and turtles. Over 50% of the island's surface is classified under the Natura 2000 Network, and is especially rich in endemic flora and fauna and a wide diversity of habitat within which almost 50 plant species have been identified. Although far from accessible, the cliffs are favoured by Cory's shearwater as a nesting ground. Common tern is also found here, along with the Azorean woodpigeon.

Today, with its airport that from a distance looks like the newly laid main street of a town, the centuries-long quasi-isolation of the island is ended. Now the island plays a part in the affairs of all the Azores, its economy largely founded on **cattle rearing**, **cheese production** and such tourism as it can get.

> **CORVO SUMMIT**
>
> The highest point in Corvo, to the south of the volcanic crater, is Morro dos Homens, at 718m (2356ft). The entire island was formed by the collapse of a volcano, forming a *caldeira*. Known on the island as 'Caldeirão', the crater is 300m (984ft) deep and has a diameter of 2km (1 mile), and is often shrouded in mist.

Below: *To keep free-range cattle together, the matriarchs of the group are often hobbled to prevent them from comfortably walking any distance.*

Below: *The view across the Atlantic from Ponta Delgada, Faial, to the island of Corvo.*

For too long Corvo has suffered from a reputation of being difficult to access: flights are infrequent even at the height of summer, and bad weather can prevent flights from landing or boats from crossing the intervening 15 nautical miles from Flores. But there are long periods, too, when Corvo presents no such problems, and with a contingency period built into a visit (if possible), there can be many worse things than temporary confinement on Corvo.

VILA DO CORVO **

As the boat arrives at Corvo it is invariably greeted by islanders awaiting the arrival of essential products. Most of the people live in Vila do Corvo, where simple architecture dominates, although the black stone façades of the houses have largely been painted white. As if depending on one another for support and shelter, the houses huddle together along the cobbled streets. The only road leads up above the village to the pastures for the cows, and then onward to the rim of the crater.

CALDEIRÃO ***

When the top of the volcano that forms Corvo collapsed it formed a huge crater, called Caldeirão, which today has a lake at the bottom, and walls lined with moss. This is a good

place to study the geological history of the island with consecutive layers of lava and ash, but it is also an immensely satisfying place just to sit and relax, and gaze out across nature's beauty. It is possible to take a car much of the way, but better, if time allows, to walk the 6km (3 miles) to **Monte Gordo** where the rim of the crater is reached.

Corvo at a Glance

During the summer months there are flights to Corvo from Terceira three times a week; from Faial likewise, and from Flores twice a week. During the winter months, this frequency reduces a little. In summer it is possible to arrange to visit Corvo from Flores on one of a number of small boats that cross to the islands. But be sure to check return times from Corvo. Hotels on Flores have contacts with boat owners and can arrange trips.

It is really all about walking. There are many private cars, and someone may drive visitors to the crater. But the main thing is to allow enough time to explore on foot.

Guesthouse Comodoro, Caminho do Areeiro s/n, Ilha do Corvo, 9980-034 Corvo, tel/fax: 292 596 128. Air conditioning, cable TV and free Internet in every room. Clean, simple, friendly.

Restaurante Trainera, Rua da Matriz (near the harbour), 9980 Corvo, tel: 292 596 207. If it swims in the sea, it is likely to find a place here, on someone's plate. All very fishy, in the nicest possible sense. But check before leaving for Corvo that it will be open, in case it isn't and you need to take your own refreshments.

There is understandably much less walking opportunity on Corvo than on the other islands, but the main feature is the ramble up to the island's *caldeira*, a vast crater of peace and tranquillity. Other walks are available, and the tourist board has produced a couple of leaflets describing walks. These can usually be picked up at any of the tourist offices, but for certain in Faial (Horta).

Tourist Information
Flores: Rua Dr Armas da Silveira, 9970-331 Santa Cruz das Flores, tel: 292 592 369, fax: 292 592 846. There is no tourist office on Corvo.

Travel Tips

Tourist Information

The Azores Tourism Association is a non-profit making partnership between the public and private sectors; its aim is to promote the Azores region as a tourist destination, and to boost the flow of tourists in order to contribute to a sustainable development of the Autonomous Region.

The UK-based **Portuguese Trade and Tourism Office** is at 1 Belgrave Square, London SW1X 8PP, tel: 020 7201 6666, fax: 020 7201 6633, email: tourism.london@portugalglobal.pt website: www.visitportugal.com

The **Regional Directorate of Tourism for the Azores** is based on Faial: Direcção Regional de Turismo, Rua Ernesto Rebelo 14, 9900-112 Horta, Faial, tel: 292 200 500, fax: 292 200 501, email: acoresturismo@mail.telepac.pt website: www.drtacores.pt They have branch offices on all the islands, and produce an excellent series of books and maps about each island. The website also lists annually updated lists of approved family hotels (*pensão*) and accommodation in rural areas.

Tourist Offices

São Miguel
Delegação de Turismo de São Miguel, Avenue Infante D. Henrique, 9500-150 Ponta Delgada, tel: 296 285 743 or 296 285 152, fax: 296 282 211, email: info.turismo@drt.raa.pt

Terceira
Rua Direita 70/74, 9700-066 Angra do Heroísmo, tel: 295 213 393, fax: 295 212 922, email: turter@mail.telepac.pt

Tourist Information Desks

Faial
Rua Vasco da Gama, 9900-017 Horta, tel: 292 292 237, fax: 292 292 006.

Flores
Rua Dr Armas da Silveira, 9970-331 Santa Cruz das Flores, tel: 292 592 369, fax: 292 592 846.

Graciosa
Rua da Boavista 9, 9980-377 Santa Cruz da Graciosa, tel: 295 712 509, fax: 295 732 446.

Pico
Gare Maritima da Madalena, 9950 Madalena, Pico, tel/fax: 292 623 524.

Santa Maria
Airport, Apartado 560, 9580 Vila do Porto, tel: 296 886 355, fax: 296 882 449.

São Jorge
Rua Conselheiro Dr José Pereira 3 R/C, 9800-530 Velas, tel: 295 412 440, fax: 295 412 491.

São Miguel
Airport: Aeroporto João Paulo II, 9500 Ponta Delgada, tel: 296 284 569.

São Miguel
Furnas: Rua Frederico Moniz Pereira 14, 9675 Furnas, tel/fax: 296 584 525.

Terceira
Airport: Aerogare Civil das Lajes, 9760-251 Lajes, tel: 295 513 140, fax: 295 543 015.

Entry Requirements

The Azores, as part of Portugal, are a full member of the European Union, and nationals of other EU countries do not require a **visa** for holidays of less then three months. It is always advisable, however, to carry your passport or national identity card.

Customs

Normal European Union customs requirements apply to visitors arriving in the Azores. **Duty-free goods** are not available for travel within the EU. Under EU guidelines, travellers within the EU may bring duty-paid goods including up to 50 litres of beer, 25 litres of wine, and 800 cigarettes. Travellers from non-EU countries may bring in 200 cigarettes, 1 litre of spirits, 2 litres of wine, 50 grams of perfume and 20cc of toilet water.

Health and Safety

Portugal has reciprocal health care with the UK and other European countries. You will probably have to pay for any medical treatment, and then reclaim it later. To smooth the way you need a European Health Insurance Card available via the National Health Service. Ask at your GP's, or go online via www.nhs.uk You can get health information on tel: 0845 46 47 (24 hours, UK only) or via www.nhsdirect.nhs.uk There is also health-related travel advice available on www.dh.gov.uk/travellers or

tel: 020 7210 4850 (Mon–Fri, 09:00–17:00 UK time).

Be especially conscious of the burning effects of the sun, and not only when sunbathing or out and about, but also if you go out to sea on a boat – the sea reflects the UV rays.

The water in the Azores mainly comes from springs, and is safe to drink. Even so, some Azorean people advise sticking to bottled water for drinking purposes. If you have a propensity to sweat, be sure to drink plenty of water, and to have a bottle by your bed to drink during the night.

Electricity

Electricity is supplied at 220v using continental 2-pin plugs.

Tipping

Tipping is not generally expected; hotels and restaurants often include a service charge. But if you want to leave a tip, then 10% is about right.

Time

The Azores are GMT minus one hour, i.e. one hour *behind* the UK, and two hours *behind* mainland Europe. Clocks go forward one hour at 01:00 on the last Sunday of March, and back one hour on the last Sunday in October.

Banks, post offices and shops:

Local banks are invariably branches of the main Portuguese banks, and offer a full range of banking services including ATMs. Post offices (*Coreios*) are efficient, and postage is not expensive. Letters and cards back to the UK or mainland Europe will take 3–6 days.

Business hours are generally 09:00–13:00 and 14:00–18:00 Monday to mid-day Saturday; banking hours are 08:30–14:45 Monday–Friday.

Road Signs

Road signs are standard European signage, and are easy to decipher even if you are not familiar with them. Street names are in Portuguese.

What to Take

How long is a piece of string? As well as all your customary holiday things, there are some you should not overlook:
Sun hat – although the temperatures are not incredibly high, you will certainly be affected by the sun, so a sun hat, however ridiculous, is a good thing.
A lightweight pullover or cardigan, for use in the cool of the evening.
Sunglasses – vital; the Azorean light is magical, and intense.
Sun block – as high a factor as possible, although the best remedy is to cover up as much as you can.
Passport
Driving licence if you intend driving.

Insurance cover
Cash – travellers' cheques are old hat; all the towns and many of the villages in the Azores have banks and ATMs. The exception is Corvo. Your bank may make a charge for withdrawals from foreign banks.
Credit cards – be sure to notify your bank that the credit card is going to be used abroad; sometimes when a credit card turns up in a strange place, the payment is disallowed. Not insuperable, but embarrassing.
Binoculars – if you intend to go whale or bird-watching.
Torch – surprising how useful a torch can be if you need to find your way round a hotel in the dark, or when you go down into any of the caves.
Lightweight waterproofs – it rains in the Azores, and a lightweight waterproof jacket will be useful, and for the odd chilly day.
Medication – don't forget a sufficient supply of any regular medication you are taking, but also include a small quan-

tity of painkillers, even some tablets to relieve symptoms of a cold, and, if you react to insect bites, take some antihistamine tablets and/or cream. There are midges on all of the islands, and mosquitoes on a few. There is no malaria, but a mosquito bite can irritate for days.

Mobile Phones

International roaming (i.e. dual-band) mobile phones will work fine in the Azores, wherever there is a signal – which is most places.

Best Buys

Do *not* buy scrimshaw; it is illegal both to export it from the Azores and to import it into other European countries. The consequence of having scrimshaw found in your possession at Customs is dire.

Do buy locally made artefacts: fig pith and other wooden ornaments, jewellery, woven covers, needlework, fish-scale decorations. You can buy most of these

Conversion Chart		
From	**To**	**Multiply By**
Millimetres	inches	0.0394
Metres	yards	1.0936
Metres	feet	3.281
Kilometres	miles	0.6214
Square kilometres	square miles	0.386
Hectares	acres	2.471
Litres	pints	1.760
Kilograms	pounds	2.205
Tonnes	tons	0.984
To convert Celsius to Fahrenheit: $\times 9 \div 5 + 32$		

direct from the person making them or through a local co-operative.

Inter-island Connections

Flights between the islands invariably focus on Terceira, so that if, for example, visitors want to go from Graciosa to São Jorge, it is necessary to take a flight to Terceira and then a flight out to São Jorge. This all sounds fairly reasonable, if a little inconvenient, as the same holds true for flights between other islands in the central group. In normal circumstances luggage is checked through to your final destination, and this generally holds true. But there are times when a full aircraft may mean more baggage than they can handle. The result is that some baggage gets left behind. Some of it may go to Lisbon before coming back. It happens!

To some extent you can offset the problem of arriving at your final destination only to discover that your baggage is still where you started and not likely to arrive for another day or three – minor inconvenience for one day, but a hefty problem if it lasts much longer. If time between connecting flights permits, then rather than check baggage through to the final destination, just check it to Terceira, and reclaim it there, and go through the check-in process again. This way, if there is a problem it is discovered sooner rather than later. You may not be able to get your baggage any quicker, but at least you can plan how to handle the problem.

At all costs, do ensure that your baggage carries some form of label with your home address on it, and the address of the hotel where you are staying. It is uncertain how much truth there is in the suggestion that twice a year unclaimed baggage is auctioned off. But the best way of ensuring that your baggage reappears is to have it clearly labelled, and to report missing baggage immediately. Those responsible for tracing your baggage are generally very helpful and polite, but it will do no harm to conspicuously take the name of the person you are dealing with and a telephone number on which you can contact them.

Boats: As well as flights, inter-island connections are provided by boat, mainly between the central group of islands, by the following companies:

Açorline SA, Rua Dr Caetano de Andrade 5, 9500-037 Ponta Delgada, São Miguel, tel: 296 302 379, www.acorline.pt

Transmaçor, Rua Nova 29 R/C, Angústias, 9900-023 Horta, Faial, tel: 292 200 380, www.transmacor.pt

All islands, except Corvo, have a system of public transportation that connects daily to the other main localities.

Earthquakes

It is just over 10 years since a major earthquake occurred in the Azores, although minor

seismic tremors are experienced (not necessarily felt by the man in the street) on a regular basis. But the fact remains that this is a geologically active area, and earthquakes, while not uppermost in the minds of the local people, are nevertheless a fact of life. So, it does no harm to detail the following information from the Regional Government of the Azores: What to do, before, during and after an earthquake:

Before
• Get to know the emergency plans for the building you are staying in.
• Identify the emergency exits and check the location of fire extinguishers.
• Identify the safest areas: under an interior door jamb, in corners of support walls, under a bed or a table.
• Identify the most dangerous areas: elevators, exits to streets, near windows, mirrors or light fixtures, next to buildings, posts, retaining walls.

During
If you are inside the building:
• Seek cover under an interior door jamb, in the corner of a room, or under a substantial piece of furniture.
• Stay away from windows and mirrors.
• Don't run to the stairs.
• Don't use the elevator.
If you are in the street:
• Move as calmly as you can to an open area, as far as possible from the sea or the path of flowing water.
• If you are driving, park your car away from any buildings or substantial watercourses and stay in the car.

After
• Remain as calm as you can, and expect some aftershocks, this is normal.
• Only use the telephone in cases of emergency, e.g. major injuries. Do not use a mobile phone if you think there may be a gas leak nearby.
• Do not wander the streets to see what has happened; leave them open for emergency vehicles and services. If you are a qualified medical practitioner and think you can be of assistance, make yourself known to the emergency services.

Beware: When visiting geothermal sites with children, do keep them under close supervision; almost all of the sites are unfenced. Likewise, take care when getting in and out of the natural swimming pools around the coastlines. Basalt rock is sharp and abrasive; take jelly shoes or sandals to protect your feet.

Accommodation
Across the Azores there is a wide range of **accommodation**, with more than 70 comfortable hotels on the islands, with the exception of Corvo, where there is a luxury guesthouse. Visitors can also stay in more than 60 farmhouses, at the very heart of a family home. There are no five-star hotels, but the four-star and three-star hotels provide a high degree of comfort and facility. In the smaller hotels, there is no less a welcome, and, in general, hotel staff will go out of their way to enhance your stay and help make arrangements, as necessary.

GOOD READING

De Frias, Martins (2000). *The Azores, Isle of Blue and Green* (Ribeiro and Caravana).
Moniz, Miguel D (1999). *Azores* (ABC – Clio).
Sayers, David and Cymbron, Albano. *The Azores: Garden Islands of the Atlantic*.
Shafer, Hanno (2002). *Flora of the Azores* (Margraf Verlag, Weikersheim) – in English.
Stieglitz, Andreas (2006). *Landscapes of the Azores: a countryside guide* (Sunflower Books). Car tours and walks.

Taxis
The following is a list of English-speaking taxi drivers on the islands. If you use any of them, mention my name; it won't get you a discount, but it will reinforce their faith in humanity that when some curious journalist from England came among them, he went away and did what he said he would do!
São Miguel: José Raposo, tel: 962 408 327.
Santa Maria: Célia Moreira, tel: 962 374 403.
Terceira: José de Meneses de Lima, tel: 962 416 822.
Graciosa: Severo Rui Bettencourt Cunha, tel: 962 732 679.
São Jorge: Jorge Silveira, tel: 966 780 150.
Pico: Maria da Conceição Bernardo, tel: 963 636 075.
Faial: Terry's Cab, tel: 966 753 972.
Flores: Silvio Medina, tel: 918 804 210.

INDEX

Note: Numbers in **bold** indicate photographs